FOOTIE SHORTS

FUNNY STORIES FROM THE BEAUTIFUL GAME

STUART TURNBULL

BLACK & WHITE PUBLISHING

First published 2005
by Black & White Publishing Ltd
99 Giles Street, Edinburgh EH6 6BZ

Reprinted 2005

ISBN 1 84502 081 2

British Library Cataloguing in Publication Data:
A catalogue record for this book is available
from the British Library.

Printed and bound by DNT, Poland, EU
www.polskabook.pl

CONTENTS

ACKNOWLEDGEMENTS

Where do I begin? I have had so much help in producing this book that I am sure to miss some folk out so I begin by apologising to them!

Douglas Wilcox, Honorary Consultant in Medical Genetics at Yorkhill Hospital in Glasgow kindly wrote a letter of introduction to all my contacts and Sir Alex Ferguson, a Vice-President of the Muscular Dystrophy Campaign, endorsed my efforts and helped raise the profile of the book.

There was a period when I began to despair at the lack of new stories coming in and Robert Philip of *The Daily Telegraph* wrote an excellent article about me and about the proposed book one Saturday – the response was wonderful and suddenly the book was viable.

Russell Kyle from pmpr Public Relations voluntarily took up the challenge of bypassing some of the agents of celebrity fans and he obtained many stories for me from some weel kent figures.

My main carer, Gay Martin, spent hours filling envelopes and doing a lot of the mundane work and, not for the first time, I thank her for her infinite patience and good nature when things got difficult.

My good old Mum typed an awful lot of letters, made phone calls and sent hundreds of e-mails and generally kept me going throughout the production of the book.

The JK Cairncross Charitable Trust in Perth made a grant of £1,000 at a very early stage towards the cost of getting all the stories and I am immensely grateful to the Trustees for their faith in my project from the very start.

Finally, I cannot adequately express my thanks to all the contributors from all walks of life – without them there would be no book. Their allegiance to the beautiful game (quite often in trying circumstances as you will see from many of the stories) is commendable.

INTRODUCTION

The idea for this book came to me as I watched my local team, St Johnstone, tumble from the Scottish Premier League and my national side, Scotland, spectacularly slide down the international league of merit. If I hadn't resorted to humour, I would have slipped into despair! So, what better way to counter the doldrums than to put together a collection of humorous anecdotes from the game as seen from all the different angles? Players, referees, pundits, celebrities, commentators, managers, backroom staff and, most important of all, the ordinary fans on the terraces have their tales to tell so I decided to gather them together.

I asked for contributions and the response from most quarters was very encouraging. Some of the best quips have come from fans, young and old alike, and most, like me, are long suffering! I leave it to you, the reader, to list your favourites but, by buying my book, you have made a generous donation to the vital work of the Muscular Dystrophy Campaign to whom I have assigned all the proceeds.

There are many different forms of Muscular Dystrophy and currently there is no cure for any of them. The most progressive and most common type affects young boys. From about the age of ten, as their muscles degenerate, they have to use wheelchairs. The Muscular Dystrophy Campaign works tirelessly to provide care, services and advice for affected families and to fund research into possible therapies and cures.

Stuart Turnbull

As a charity, the Muscular Dystrophy Campaign provides people who have neuromuscular conditions, and their families, with information and advice about their condition and suggests ways in which living with MD can be made easier.

There are about sixty different types of muscular dystrophy and related neuromuscular conditions. These conditions are characterised by the loss of muscle strength, as progressive muscle wasting or nerve deterioration occurs. They are mainly inherited, can cause shortened life expectancy and there are currently no cures. The Campaign raises funds to support medical research into MD.

The Campaign also funds (with some contribution from the NHS) thirteen Care Advisors who are based in clinics around the country. They are on hand to give advice and support to people who are affected by neuromuscular conditions.

The unashamed aim of this book, apart from hopefully bringing a smile to your face, is to raise lots of royalties to donate to the Campaign to enable it, in turn, to make a real difference to its endeavours.

1

BACKROOM STAFF

Andy Coventry – Ex-Hearts FC Youth Coach

Here is one that came to mind from when I played Sunday League Football in the 1980s. One Sunday afternoon, our team, Shandon Thistle, were playing a league fixture against a team from the Deaf and Dumb Society called Albany. The game was played on a miserable dreich day up at Sighthill playing fields in Edinburgh. Sighthill is an unforgiving venue at the best of times but on days such as these it becomes even more so. On this particular day ours was the only game that was being played. I cannot recollect having substitutes on the sidelines never mind any spectators – not even the one man and his dog scenario.

Midway through the first half, our left back and centre half collided with each other, about 25 yards from goal. From the resulting collision, Albany scored what was to prove the only goal of the game giving them their first-ever victory. The two defenders started remonstrating with each other about who was to blame for the error and a heated exchange of words took place. This was interrupted by the referee who booked one and sent the other off. I intervened and asked him to reconsider as we were playing lads who were deaf and dumb and no spectators were in sight never mind earshot. He was having none of it 'Rules are rules and you'll be next!' he said. Into the second half and despite having only ten men, we had wind and slope advantage but, despite all our efforts and some inspired goal-keeping, we could not get the breakthrough and score a goal. However, we were awarded a penalty kick with a few minutes to go and you could tell by the look of despondency on the faces of the Albany team that they felt victory was about to be snatched away from them.

As our penalty kick taker was on his run-up to take the kick, all you could hear and see were groans and clenched-fist gestures, willing and encouraging their goalie to perform his heroics one more time. Unfortunately, our kicker blasted his shot over the crossbar and far into the horizon down the slope towards the main road. This was met with muted cries of jubilation and the big goalie making get-it-up-you arm and hand gestures. This was done by him bending his forearm over the other and, in his excitement, he was clearly trying to say, 'Ya ******.'

In my frustration at seeing the penalty missed and my sense of injustice at the earlier sending off, I confronted the referee to make my protestations about the goalkeeper's mumbled abuse and asking him to take similar action against him as he had done to our left back. 'Don't be stupid – he can't talk so how can he swear?' was the reply!

By this time, the goalkeeper was casually strolling in

the distance to retrieve the ball. Once again, I nipped the referee's ear by claiming that the goalkeeper was deliberately wasting time so the referee peeped his whistle several times to try and prompt him to move a bit quicker to which I said to the ref, 'Who is ****** stupid now? He cannae ****** hear neither!'

Guess what? Yes, he sent me off for dissent!

In fairness to the referee, after the game he too saw the funny side of it and never sent a report to the disciplinary committee.

And here's a quick one from my schooldays when I attended Broughton High School in Edinburgh in the early 1970s.

Our PE Teacher was the legendary Scotland and British Lions prop forward Ian 'Mighty Mouse' McLaughlin. One afternoon he took us for a game of football but before starting he told us this was to be a game with a difference. The difference was that it would be played to 'JOHN GREIG'S RULES!' 'What are John Greig's Rules?' was the response. To which his reply was, 'Easy! NO TACKLING BELOW THE KNEES!'

Desmond Thompson – Millwall Team Doctor

Thought you might like this quote from Ray Harford who was assistant coach before he sadly died in 2003.

From the dugout, watching Dennis Wise trying to win a free-kick, he said, 'Dennis went down like he had been shot by a sniper in the stand.'

Forbes Chapman – Football Administrator and Coach

I was speaking at an end of season dinner at Barclays Bank FC a few years ago and also speaking was Bob Wilson (who I know is a very, very nice man – I help him with his charity The Willow Foundation). On the first day that Bob did a job for *Sports Report* (then presented by Frank Bough), he was sent to Highbury where Arsenal were playing Southampton. Before he started the job, he asked a few friends for advice and David Coleman said, 'Prepare yourself for anything you do and if possible practise it.'

The car arrived at Highbury midway through the second half to take him to the studios in Shepherds Bush. Being very nervous, he prepared his piece as follows, 'Arsenal have enjoyed a good first half at Highbury and are leading 2–0 with 15 minutes to go from two Alan Ball goals.' He arrived at the studios and was ushered in. Frank Bough looked up and then proceeded to say the following, 'Arsenal have enjoyed a good first half at Highbury and are leading 2–0 with 15 minutes to go from two Alan Ball goals.' He said his world collapsed and, remembering what Coleman had advised, he just repeated what Frank Bough said.

What an introduction to television!

Graham Fordy – Commercial Manager, Middlesbrough Football Club

In season 1991–92 our physio was leaving the Club and

the Board were interviewing a prospective replacement recommended by the first team manager.

At this time many things were changing in the medical world due to the awareness of Aids and the importance of handling open wounds with care. Football Clubs even had to change from large team baths to individual baths and showers to meet new health requirements.

The physio that was leaving had taken the new rules to the extreme and wore rubber gloves on all occasions. Every time he ran onto the pitch prior to attending the injured players he pulled on a pair of rubber gloves. If a player went for treatment prior to or after training he always pulled on a fresh pair of rubber gloves for each player. Even if he was to massage an injured player the rubber gloves were always pulled on. This had become a standing joke at the Club and the players were always wary of what was about to happen next.

At the end of the interview with his prospective replacement when he had been asked the normal question, 'Why are you leaving your present club and what appeals to you about Middlesbrough Football Club.', checking off qualifications, etc. etc., the Chairman knowing the rubber glove situation paused and said, 'This may seem a strange question to ask but I would like you to answer it honestly. Do you wear gloves?' The interviewee paused, looked round the table at those present, rubbed his chin and replied, 'Only in the winter when it is cold, Chairman.' Everyone connected to the Club burst out laughing and the successful candidate still does not know why.

Les Seagress – Ex-Physio

A Western League match in 1980s. A young man who was, shall we say, rather small in stature, was having his first game for the first team. He could not have had a worse possible start. In the first half everything that he tried he made a complete mess of.

At half-time the manager came into the dressing room with the match ball under his arm. He walked over to the lad and said, 'Stand up, son.' He then placed the ball on the floor in front of the lad and got down on the floor behind the ball. 'What are you doing, Boss?' the lad asked. 'I am trying to see if you can see over the top of the bloody ball'!

Muir Stratford – Director of Watford, 1971–90

I was a Director of Watford Football Club from 1971 to 1990. I was already on the Board when my friend Elton John joined the Board, as a Director and then Chairman. We persuaded Graham Taylor to join us as Manager in 1977 and then went from Division 4 in 1977 to finish second in the old First Division in 1983 to Liverpool.

During my time on the Board, we had three Board meetings in Europe, in Vienna, Paris and Milan. I wonder how many other Clubs can emulate this and this was in the days of all Directors being non-executive and being a Director was a hobby.

My anecdote relates to the Vienna visit. We played West Ham on Saturday afternoon and we all left by minibus for Heathrow immediately after the final whistle (with wives). Upon arrival in Vienna, we went to the Hotel Bristol and were having dinner in the restaurant when our Chairman who had been giving a concert wafts in to the restaurant dressed just as you would have expected Wolfgang Amadeus Mozart to look all those years ago, and he always said he wanted to keep a low profile!

Steve Finch – Club Photographer, Crewe Alexandra

ALL FOR THE SAKE OF THREE POINTS
Having travelled on the team coach to away games for a number of years, one trip still sticks in my mind this being the away game at Torquay while we were in Division Four. We left Crewe early, as in those days an overnight stop was not heard of, and made our way down the M6. Having travelled for no more than 15 minutes the driver informed us of the fact that the coach was overheating and he needed to stop to top up the water level. Having done this, we thought that this would be the last stop before we got to Torquay. How wrong we were as we had to stop many more times before we reached our destination. On each occasion, the coach was shrouded in steam – this being due to the fact that the thermostat had jammed. On getting to Torquay, the driver took the coach to be repaired while the game was on.

After the game, which Crewe won, the players boarded the coach for the trip home. All started well until we reached Exeter where some of the players at the back told the driver that they could smell something burning. He then pulled in to the next available services and examined the rear of the coach and informed us that a fan belt was breaking. He had a spare but had a real problem – he did not have a spanner to fit the nut holding the pulley. Armed with this information, we then started stopping passing cars and asking if they had one which would help him out. Finding none, the next point of call was at the petrol station on site where spanners were on display. On asking if we could borrow one to complete our task, he was told that, if he wanted a spanner, we would have to buy a complete set. With this rebuttal he then returned to the coach. A passing motorist saw our problem and let us have his spanner to replace the belt with his help. The journey from that point onwards was uneventful and we returned to Gresty Road over 13 hours after we had left. Thank goodness we won!

Trevor Atkinson – Middlesbrough Tour Guide

I am a tour guide at the ground and, inevitably, we get a number of ribald or naive comments from those we are guiding. I give below a couple.

We have an ex-player, now a radio pundit with Century FM, whose name you may be aware of, Bernie Slaven, who famously bared his bum in Binns' store window following Middlesbrough's defeat of Manchester United at Old Trafford a couple of seasons ago. Whilst taking groups around, we show a selection of international shirts worn by some of our players past and present and have one of Bernie's. This is a Republic of Ireland shirt and he is a Scotsman. I usually make some comment about, regardless of nationality, whilst Jack Charlton was the manager, he could always find a way of proving you were of Irish descent. On this particular occasion, one of our visitors beat me to the end of my storyline with, 'Of course he qualifies – he owns an Irish Setter.'

A more moving story occurred when I was taking a group of seven and eight year olds around the stadium at the time that Brazil were playing the World Cup final in Japan in 2002. We followed their progress in a sketchy way, as many of the public spaces and private rooms have TV monitors which were all switched on. We had just reached a display which includes a pair of Juninho's boots. Innocently, a little girl asked, 'So is he playing in his bare feet today then?'

Tom Spence – Public Address Announcer, Tonbridge AFC

A number of years ago I had a late-afternoon appointment at the dentist which involved injections to freeze my gums. A few hours later, I was at 'The Angels' Longmead Stadium for an evening game. Despite the discomfort in my mouth, I was still able to do the announcing and give out the team changes etc. This included informing the crowd that 'Tonight's match is sponsored by Brook Decorations Ltd.' For the sponsors benefit, I made this announcement several times over the PA. After the game and also at work the next day, I was asked who the Chinese firm who sponsored the game was? My announcements had sounded like 'Blook Decalations'!

2

CELEBRITY FANS

Andy Cameron – Comedian and Rangers Fan

It was back in 1978 and the venue was Eindhoven. It was a European tie and PSV had held Rangers to a 0–0 draw at Ibrox. We had played quite well at Ibrox and were unlucky not to score. The return leg turned out to be a bit of a cracker. I was at the game and we were rocked when PSV rattled one in to the net. Time? 22 seconds. Aye, that's right 22 bloody seconds!

I went to the loo at half time and in comes this big bear (pardon the pun!) bedecked in Rangers colours and covered in badges. Literally hundreds of badges. Put it this way, if he walked past a magnet shop, he would have been pulled in! He walks up to the wall gets ready for a pee and utters a line that reduced me to tears of laughter. He looked at me and with a deadly straight face said, '22 seconds. The bastards started before we were ready.'

The story had a happy ending mind you, the Teddy Bears went on to win 3–2.

The next one was Wembley 1967. Aye, that was the game where we took on England, then the World Champions, and beat them 3–2. Whit a gemme!

Anyway, midway through the first half I was burstin' for a pee. We were packed in and getting to the toilet was going to be difficult, if not impossible. I pointed out my predicament to the guy standing beside me and he said, 'Just pee in the pocket of the guy in front of you.'

I said I couldn't do that and, anyway, he would notice.

The guy then says to me, 'Well you didn't!'

Aye, fitba matches are magic.

The road to Wembley was a bit like a geography lesson for me. I was about nine and going to London on the train with my dad and his pals. Where does the geography come in? I knew we were in Motherwell when the cry went up, 'The kerry-oot is finished.'

Great gemme, intit?

Billy Connolly – Comedian and Celtic Fan

I was sitting in a film studio waiting to be called on to the set and there were some magazines lying around. I am one of these people who will stick my nose into any magazine and see what's what. This turned out to be a French magazine. Most of it didn't mean too much to me but I pulled up short when I came across a certain picture. Here was really cool looking guy complete with a green beard! I thought to myself, 'That'll do me, nicely.' Pamela, my wife, thought I was bonkers. Mind you, nothing new in that, is there? I mean a green beard!

My mind was made up. In jig time the moustache and beard were a nice shade of green. Let me say, right now, it was nothing to do with my abiding love for Celtic Football Club. I just thought I looked real cool.

Next thing was take in a game. Off I went to Celtic Park with my pal. I love going to a game. The way my work schedule is, I don't get to as many matches as I would like to. This particular Saturday, it was against Aberdeen and we usually do pretty good against the Dons.

The Club treats me really well and they always allow me to park in the school at the entrance to the stadium. It's only about a 60-yard walk and I always sign my fair share of autographs and pose for pictures with the fans. It's the least you can do. I hate these celebs that do the 'I don't do autographs' routine. Anyway, I'm walking up to the ground and then I'm under siege to sign assorted things. There are a few comments about the green beard and 'tache but one guy just knocks me stone dead with a killer line. Here's me thinking I'm King Cool with the green beard and this guy says, 'Hey, Big Yin, huv ye been eatin' a pie and peas?' He reduced me to tears.

That's the thing about Glasgow and the natives of this fine city – they have a knack of bringing you right down to earth.

The game was a bit of a belter, too. Celtic rattled in seven.

Earlier this season, I managed to get to one of Celtic's

early European ties. It was against Kauness. I drove down to Glasgow with my son Jamie from my home up near Aberdeen. I was meeting up with my Celtic-mad pal again and we parked in Albion Street in the Merchant City to get a bite to eat. I was in my big yellow Land Rover and I left my bag with all my stuff lying in the back. Needless to say, some wee tea leaf broke into the car and nicked my bag. I was left in my T-shirt and denims.

That night I was to go on to the park at half-time and present the Kauness people with a cheque. Their young star striker had been killed in a car crash and the Celtic supporters and club had raised money for the lad's wife and young family. Anyway, I had to sprint round the shops and buy myself some new gear, sharpish!

I never had time to report the theft to the local polis. As we came down for the obligatory half-time pie, two cops got hold of my pal and told him they had recovered all my stuff. It came as a bit of shock they had found it as I hadn't even told them I had lost it!

At the end of the game we went to London Road polis station to collect the bag and nothing had been touched. Some guy had seen the thief look in the bag and throw it in some bushes at the bottom of High Street and the kind man had called the cops. One big polis quipped, 'Mind you, Billy, who the hell is going to buy a green-and-white striped suit in your size?'

Ah, Glasgow is full of comedians.

Fred MacAulay –
Radio Presenter and St Johnstone Fan

I was never a particularly good footballer. I was enthusiastic but lacked skills. More importantly, I lacked confidence. Despite that, I used to turn out to watch a few of my schoolmates who played for a team in the Perth Juvenile League and on the odd occasion I'd get a strip and be brought on for a few minutes towards the end if the team were far enough ahead! More often than not though, I'd be on the sidelines for the full 90 minutes.

Home matches were played on The South Inch at Perth and prior to The Annual Perth Show, chestnut fencing was erected around the perimeter of the pitches. This meant that if the ball went out of play and over the fences then the ball boy (i.e. me in my strip, waiting to get on as a substitute) had to run all the way down the length of the pitch, out of the fenced off area, get the ball, kick it back over the fence and then run all the way back.

I have to say that my heart sank as the team manager said to me just after I'd retrieved the ball one time, 'Just stay on that side of the fence, Fred, for when the ball comes out again.' Needless to say, this didn't do my confidence much good and pretty well signalled the end of my football career!

Thanks to that manager, I've become a decent skier and golfer.

Jack Ryder – Actor and Ex-Eastenders (team unknown)

For nine years I lived on a road which was right next to a park. Every day, after school, I would get together with a group of about eight friends and play football till there were stars in the sky. Over the years, I developed as quite a nippy right winger with pace and a good right foot. This was what I wanted to do. I wanted to play football!

I found out that Charlton Athletic organized summer trials for kids who hadn't been spotted and it gave kids the opportunity to train with professional coaches. I felt that this would be my way in and was utterly determined to get on the course and show my ability. I never had the opportunity to play for a football team because, as my parents were divorced, each weekend I travelled to be with my father. This course then was my best chance to find a way into football.

Two days before the summer coaching began I was playing football outside my house. The ball was kicked across the street. As I ran across the street, I looked to the left but as I looked to the right I slipped and a car which knocked me down ran over my ankle. I spent the next six months using crutches! That was the end of my football chances.

I was around about 13 when the above incident happened and my dreams were shattered. Possibly I would not have made it professionally but . . . I wonder!

John Francome – Jockey and Swindon Town Fan

A traffic warden who was a Swindon Town supporter died and was taken to the mortuary. When the mortician pulled back to sheet to reveal the body, he was startled to hear the traffic warden say, 'It's OK, I am still alive.'

The mortician replies, 'I am very sorry but I have started to write out your ticket.' and shot him!

Rod Stewart – Musician and Celtic Fan

I have many memories of Scottish football. Some brilliant, some not so good. Some with the Scotland side and some with Celtic.

I first met the Scotland team around 1973. A journalist pal in Scotland, Russell Kyle, (also a good Celtic supporter!) had invited me up and had set up the chance for me to visit the team down at their training headquarters at Largs.

I was as nervous as hell. 'Maggie May' had launched my career and I suppose I had started the climb to the top of my own career in the music business, but I was really excited at the prospect of meeting the team. It was the lead up to the '74 World Cup in Germany and my two footballing heroes were in the squad –Denis Law and Kenny Dalglish. The Lawman was THE man for me at the time. If I remember rightly, I wanted to buy him something as a keepsake of the meeting so I arrived with the biggest telly I could get my hands on!

We drove down to the seaside town of Largs and, by the time we arrived, the players were all in bed for an afternoon rest as they had a game that night. Wee Willie Ormond was the manager at the time and he had left the hotel to go for a walk. We managed to get Kenny Dalglish down from his room and I think he thought it was a bit of a wind-up. But when he saw me standing there, he shot back upstairs and got the entire team out of their beds and down to the lounge to meet us.

The players weren't sure how Willie Ormond would react to them being out of their beds, so we kept the visit to reasonably brief 20 minutes or so. And they were all back in their rooms by the time he got back.

But I was like a star-struck wee boy in among so many of the guys I loved to watch on the park. Billy Bremner was the captain at the time and he was a smashing wee guy – hard as nails on the park but a great guy off it. Meeting Denis was a sheer joy. Oh, and I think he liked the telly.

Another great day I had was when we visited Celtic Park and met the legendary Jock Stein. The players had just finished training and Big Jock threw the ball which I caught on my thigh and started doing a few keepy-uppies. I think he was impressed. Russell told him I had signed professional forms when I was a 16-year-old at Brentford so I could play a bit. I still play as often as I can.

Anyway, wee Jimmy Johnstone asked us to meet him and some of the Celtic lads in a pub not too far from Celtic Park. If my memory serves me right, it was called the Duke of Tourraine. We sunk a right few beers that afternoon. Incidentally, wee Jinky is not a bad singer at all!

I played the Apollo in Glasgow that night and it was one of the best gigs ever. I think it was because I was such a high from meeting the Celtic boys in the afternoon. I used to do six gigs in Glasgow in those days – three nights on stage, one night off and then another three.

I love Glasgow, and I love Scotland and the Scots. To this day, I still take in as many Celtic and Scotland games as I can. In fact, it's only now that I am managing to put the disappointment of Seville behind me.

As for the future of the game, there are a lot of good young players just beginning to break through and I think Scotland will soon be a force to reckon with again.

3

COMMENTATORS AND PUNDITS

Alan Hansen – BBC Pundit and Ex-Internationalist

A famous Liverpool player who was Irish went into a Pizza Hut and ordered a 12-inch pizza.

The waitress asked if he wanted it cut into six pieces or eight pieces.

He replied, 'Cut it into six pieces – I could never eat eight!'

Albert Sewell – BBC *Match of the Day* Statistician

During the last *Match of the Day* series that Des Lynam presented, he liked, whenever possible, to close the show with a 'Man of the Day', featuring a player who had scored a special goal, a goalkeeper for some outstanding saves or, maybe, a manager for an inspired substitution.

One afternoon, as the 'team' assembled in the viewing room to watch the matches that would make that night's highlights, I mentioned that Premiership goal scoring that season was running at a record high. So what did we get from our three main matches? Three nil–nils! Cue for Des's closing link, 'Man of the Day – our man Albert.'

Bob Wilson – BBC *Football Focus* presenter, Arsenal and Scotland Goalkeeper and Arsenal Goalkeeping Coach 1975–2003

I was presenting *Football Focus* 'live' when my editor told me in my earpiece, 'Bob, we have just heard Joe Jordan's fit for today's game. Try and slip it into the news straightaway.' Without batting an eyelid, I immediately looked into the camera and came out with, 'Team news just in. We've just heard Joe Jordan has just pissed a late fatness test.' Of course, I had meant 'passed a late fitness test'.

Eamonn O'Neal – Executive Producer Regional Programmes, Granada Television

Just over 10 years ago, I co-presented BBC *GMR Sport* with Jimmy Wagg. Jimmy's gone from strength to strength as a sports journalist – because he was always good. On the other hand, I didn't really know what I was doing. After one local game finished I announced on the radio that we'd be talking to three lads from Stockport, Ted, Mack and Ernie. I realised I wasn't cut out for sports broadcasting when Jimmy pointed out that it was actually Stockport's new signing, Ted McInerney!

That was a couple of weeks after I'd asked a news-reader, 'How long is this 24-hour rail strike likely to last?' I was sacked soon afterwards!

Nowadays I work for Granada Television in Manchester and do a bit of radio with Jimmy Wagg on a Sunday morning (but thankfully nothing to do with football!).

Gary Lineker – BBC *Match of the Day* presenter and Ex-Leicester City, Everton, Barcelona, Tottenham Hotspur, Nagoya Grampus 8 and England Striker

I once played a game at Birmingham. After the match, we were leaving the field when someone spat at one of our players in the tunnel. Unfortunately, my team mate spat back. The following week we had a team meeting. The manager, Gordon Milne, said that a report had been received from the police about the incident. He then said, 'This sort of behaviour is unacceptable and the next time somebody spits at you, you just have to swallow it.'

Hazel Irvine – BBC *Grandstand* Presenter

I spent many happy years around Scottish football grounds and perhaps my favourite weekends were Scottish Cup weekends. I had the pleasure of visiting many smaller grounds, including one very memorable trip to Burntisland Shipyard FC in Fife, where we were looked after royally on what was a truly Baltic afternoon!

That visit stands out, but my most vivid memories are of Gayfield, home of Arbroath FC. The occasion was the eve of the 1993 Scottish Cup quarter final as Arbroath geared up to face the mighty Rangers at home. Arbroath's manager at that time was Danny McGrain, who'd taken over in November '92 and had instantly acquired cult status amongst the fans. Hundreds of them donned false whiskers and so was born McGrain's 'Bearded Army'. These foot soldiers were quite a sight and sang their hearts out throughout games.

Given the fact that Danny was also a Celtic legend and he was guiding a (pre-reconstruction) Div 2 side against his auld adversaries, this tie captured the imagination in so many ways. In fact, we decided to broadcast our Friday evening preview programme, *Friday Sportscene*, LIVE from the Gayfield boardroom the night before the game. Well, what an evening we had!

For a start, this boardroom was all of 20 feet long by 15 feet wide – at the very most – and somehow what seemed like a cast of thousands all managed to squeeze in. There were, in truth, about 60 people shoehorned together, including half of the Bearded Army, Danny himself, the-then Rangers boss Walter Smith, the Arbroath board, their friends and families – oh, yes, and an outside broadcast crew!

Amazingly, it all went out live with very few glitches. The Bearded Army sang, on cue, and reasonably in tune! Walter and Danny produced some terrific banter. We made features based along the old 'High Rollers v Part

Timers' line. It was one of those programmes that I felt really conveyed the terrific sense of excitement ahead of a David-and-Goliath-type cup game. It was genuinely great fun.

Then, after the broadcast was all over, Rob Maclean, Chick Young and myself were whisked off into town by the Arbroath board members and invited into what felt like every pub in the town! All of the talk was about the football. 'It's a big ask, but it's 11 men against 11 men. You just never know . . .' So much chat. So much anticipation. So much to look forward to. The enthusiasm was infectious and intoxicating. Literally. Suffice to say we were made extremely welcome! My memories thereafter are somewhat hazy . . .

Next day, the Arbroath dream didn't come true. Goliath had the final say. Rangers won 3—0. No disgrace in that scoreline, of course. Indeed, there was a palpable sense of pride from the Bearded Army at having reached the quarters.

It's a cup tie I'll never forget. The build-up encapsulates how football, and sport generally, can enthuse a whole community and bring it together even for a short time. That, for me, is the magic of the Cup.

Jim Reynolds – *The Herald* Sports Editor

Ex-Scotland manager Tommy Docherty was asked one day what his opinion of the press was. He replied, 'There's a place for the press in football but they haven't dug it yet!'

Jimmy Hill – Footballer, Coach, BBC *Match of the Day* Presenter and Sky Sports Pundit

My worst moment in over 40 years on TV was when I was referring to an international rugby player. Concentrating hard on getting the name right, not an easy one I might add, I hit the bull's eye with 'Nigel Stammer Smith' – three names all correct! Sadly and embarrassingly I ended with 'who had seven craps as a scrum half in England'. One of the joys of live television.

Jimmy Wagg – BBC Radio Manchester Sport Presenter

After 15 years with the Beeb, I've learned to stay pretty calm when it gets a bit fraught. As I've got older though, my producers invariably get younger. (The current incumbent is about 12!)

I was working with one lad who was like a coiled spring, he got so wound up. He asked me how I stayed so calm and I told him that, when the pressure started to build, I just turned off the computer and went home for a bit of a 'romantic interlude' with my missus. He was a bit incredulous but I told it worked for me and he should consider it.

A few days later I saw him looking very bright and breezy and he told me he'd taken my advice for dealing with stress. I asked if it had worked for him, to which he replied, 'It certainly did and haven't you got a lovely house!'

BOOM BOOM.

John Motson – BBC Commentator

Early in the 1970s, very few people had colour televisions and black and white sets were the order of the day. I had received a complaint from a viewer whom I decided to appease during my Match of the Day live commentary from Old Roker Park Ground. I said, 'For the benefit of those with black and white television, Spurs are in the yellow shirts!'

Mike Ingham – BBC Football Correspondent

Over the last 15 years or so, Alan Green and I have been fortunate to commentate together on many of the big football occasions for BBC Radio. During this period there have been some eventful penalty shoot-outs to decide games – most of them involving England.

Alan and I always take turns starting or finishing matches and the way it works is, if we get to penalties, whoever has started the game describes the first penalty and after that we alternate. The team I describe taking the penalties always end up losing! It began with Pierce and Waddle for England in the 1990 World Cup – continued with Baggio for Italy in the 1994 final and then, at Euro '96, after I had described the Spanish misses against England in the quarter final, inevitably I was at the microphone when Southgate stepped up for his spot kick in the semifinal. Then, two years later, it was yours truly again for Ince and Batty against Argentina – so, when we got to last season's Champions League Final in Manchester, as soon as we knew that I would be commentating on the Juventus penal-ties, we said on the air, prematurely, AC Milan will win the Cup – and they duly did.

Alan and I have now made a pact that if, in future tournaments, we are commentating on England in a penalty shoot-out, it will be irrelevant whose turn it is to start and finish – I will always commentate on the opposition penalties!

Murray McGregor – Radio Tay Presenter

Dick Donnelly, Radio Tay's Sports Presenter, was on a golf outing with Dundee United at Gleneagles and, despite Jim McLean's well-known dislike of the press, they were invited. Dick had been struggling with ill-ness and only intended to go as a spectator – as he had a patch on one eye, the lids having been stitched together. Despite that, he was talked into playing. Upon reaching a bunker towards the end of his round, Dick collapsed – and the next thing he knew, he was spread-eagled across the 16th tee with players coming in from all directions to see how he was.

He picked himself up to promptly hook a four wood well wide of the green, where it struck a bush, tricked through the heather, in between bunkers . . . and rolled in for a hole in one! He still has the certificate to prove it.

Dick was asked to do a rugby report for Borders Radio. He covered a Dundee High School FP match at Mayfield – they were playing a Borders club. In true professional fashion, his half-time and full-time summaries included the scoreline. Unfortunately, no-one had advised him that a new points system was in operation and a try had been increased to five points. The rugby fans listening in the Borders must have been shocked when they read the real score in the newspapers the next morning!

I was at McDiarmid Park, Perth, for Radio Tay. The game, contested between St Johnstone and Brechin, was sitting at 3-0 to Saints with less than a minute remaining. Mixu Paateleinen had scored twice for St Johnstone. Then, as I was jotting down a few last-minute notes, I looked up to see Mixu rise and head home another goal. A Mixu hat-trick – that's the line, the story.

Suddenly Brechin ran up the park and netted a consolation and then the final whistle blew. And immediately he got the cue from the studio, 'Full time at McDiarmid Park, here's Murray McGregor . . .' I kicked off the match report, announcing that Mixu would be making all the headlines with his three-goal show etc. . . . So, the final score from Perth, St Johnstone 4 Brechin City 1.'

Then, a St Johnstone official, having heard my live report, pointed out to that Mixu's third 'goal' had been ruled offside – he had only scored twice – and that the final score was actually 3–1!

Norman Frisby – Press Officer, Granada Television, 1959–88

THE DAY I CAPTAINED UNITED

I worked at Granada Television in Manchester in 1960s when we made a weekly football preview show *Sports Outlook* with journalist Gerry Loftus, looking ahead to Saturday's fixtures.

I was going home one evening, every inch the desk-bound businessman – balding, bespectacled, best-suited, collared and tied. As I pushed through the glass door of TV Centre, a small boy ran out of the group of autograph hunters who usually gathered there. 'Hey, mister,' he yelled. 'Are you David Erd?' 'No,' I muttered, in total bewilderment. 'Er, no.' and made for the car park.

It was only when I got home and looked at the TV page of the *Manchester Evening News* that I realised David Hurd, captain of Manchester United, was being interviewed on *Sports Outlook* that evening.

My chest swelled with pride! Mistaken for a legendary giant of Old Trafford, indeed . . .

Peter McLean – Public Relations

Brian Clough is working at the Notts Forest ground and has taken a couple of guests to the boardroom. He lifts the phone and calls downstairs to the catering department. He asks for teas, coffees and biscuits for him and his guests. He is told they are busy but they would be with him in 10 minutes.

Twenty minutes later, by then annoyed, Mr Clough calls and asks where the hell his teas, coffees and biscuits were. The conversation went like this:

Clough: 'I ordered teas, coffees and biscuits to the boardroom some 20 minutes ago and they are still not here. Where the hell are they?'

Catering department: 'We are very busy down here.'

Raging Clough: 'Do you know who I am?'

Catering department voice: 'Yes, you are Mr Clough manager of the club. Do you know who you are speaking to, Mr Clough?'

Furious Clough: 'No, I have no idea.'

Catering department voice: 'Well f*** off then!' and then hangs up the phone.

Rodney Marsh – Ex-Fulham, QPR, Manchester City and England Player and Sky Sports Pundit

People often ask me why I only got nine caps for England. The following story is a true one that has been told by many an after dinner speaker – but it actually happened to me.

England were playing Northern Ireland in the Home Nations Championship and, before the game, Sir. Alf Ramsey gave his team talk. Alf like me was a cockney but he had had elocution lessons and now spoke very posh. He began his team talk in the dressing room, 'Today we are playing Northern Ireland. They have many great players – Pat Jennings, Terry Neill, Derek Dougan and of course Georgie Best. If we are going to win today, we must work hard as a team. I've told you

before how important it is that you work hard in international football. Rodney – you in particular must
work harder. In fact, if I think you aren't trying hard
enough, I'll pull you off at half-time.'

'Blimey,' I said, 'at Man City we only get a cup of tea
and an orange.'

I was never picked for England again.

Russell Kyle – Public Relations and Celtic Fan

I was at the Celtic v St Johnstone game at the end of
season 1997–98. It was a glorious day weather-wise
and it was also a huge day in the history of Celtic Football Club. There was so much hype surrounding the
game – victory against the men from Perth would
ensure Celtic won the Premier League Championship
and, more importantly for many Celtic fans, was the
fact that a win would stop deadly rivals Rangers doing
10-in-a-row. Had Celtic lost, Rangers would have
beaten the Parkhead side's world record of nine titles
in a row! To say it was tense was a bit like saying Pele
could play a wee bit!

Anyway, I set off from home in Bearsden, to pick
up longtime pal Billy Connolly from the Hilton Hotel
in Glasgow's city centre. On the drive into town, every-
where seemed to be a sea of green and white. It was
obvious driving down Maryhill Road, that the natives
had been already heavily into the bevvy. The atmosphere was superb.

Since we were invited to the Directors' Box and
Board Room, the code of dress was strictly shirt and

tie. At least that's what was clearly stated on our invite. Unfortunately, the invite was sent to me and I never thought to mention the tie rule to Billy! I met him and he was wearing a rather fetching Burberry suit. Subtle it ain't. But what do you expect from a man who has at times had a green beard and a purple beard? Better still, he wore a superb black designer T-shirt instead of the obligatory shirt and tie. The man looked King of Cool. There was no way I was going to mention shirt and tie – to be honest, I'd forgotten all about it.

The people at Celtic love Billy as much as he loves the club. They kindly provided us with a VIP car park pass that is just about a 60-yard walk to the main entrance. Mind you, that wee walk can sometimes take an age, as the Big Yin signs autographs and has his photograph taken dozens of times with fans. Once inside, normality returns. The shirt and tie rule never crossed my mind, until big Gary, who greets the board-room guests, appeared at my side and whispered, 'I don't think Mr McCann will be too pleased with Billy's mode of dress.'

Neither of us had met Fergus McCann before but I knew Fergus was a real stickler for the rule book. I managed to get a quiet word with Billy who, to his credit was slightly embarrassed. Mind you, he did come out with a great line. 'The last time I wore a shirt and tie was on my First Communion day!'

Anyway, a couple of minutes later in came Fergus. By sheer luck (was that bad luck?) I was the first person he met as he opened the door at the tunnel end of the boardroom. I said, as I shook his hand, 'Nice to meet you, Mr McCann. I believe you are not too happy with Billy Connolly's mode of dress?'

Fergus turned round to survey the boardroom and headed off to meet the Big Yin.

Billy sees him coming and shouts, 'Fergus, how are you? Lovely to meet you but what kind of football club are you running here? I took my tie off two seconds ago and some b*****d's gone off with it!'

Fergus and the whole Board Room erupted into fits of laughter.

The tie was never mentioned and never has been since. To be fair Billy always wears one now and always gives it away to a supporter at the end of the game.

Oh, as a bonus, Celtic stuffed the Saints 2-0. Larsson (who else?) and Bratbaak were the scorers. Title secured.

The journey back into the city centre was an eventful one. We stayed at the ground until about an hour-and-a-half after the game ended and then headed off. We opened the front doors and it seemed the 60,000 crowd had just moved from inside the stadium to the car park outside the ground. Absolute bedlam! The normal 15-minute journey took us over an hour during which Billy posed for more photographs, signed hundreds of autographs and said, 'Hello Maw!' to bemused mums as mobiles were thrust into his hand.

We had reached the Gallowgate when one huge bear of a man spotted Billy in the car. The big man had obviously had his head in the lager trough all day! He staggered towards us with a pie supper in his hands. 'Billy, will you sign this?'

All he had in his hand was the pie supper so Billy said: 'Sign what, big man?'

'This,' he said as he turned the pie supper upside down and handed Billy the now empty tray.

A day to remember for a whole load of reasons.

4

PLAYERS

Lorenzo Amoruso – Blackburn Rovers

The scene is the Thistle Hotel in the heart of Glasgow. The occasion is the launch of my book, *L. A. Confidential*. There is a huge dinner attended by 848 Rangers supporters, a friend of mine who is crazy about Celtic and one of my old Italian club managers, Claudio Ranieri. They both wanted to share what was a special night for me. I wanted the book done while everything was so fresh in my memory. I had invited all my Rangers team mates and a lot of football people I had met over the years. I also wore a kilt for the night. I love Scotland and all things Scottish. Yes, even haggis!

Claudio did not have great command of the English language at the time. It was also his first visit to Scotland, never mind Glasgow. I introduced him to a group of my Scottish friends who, in typically warm Glaswegian fashion, welcomed him to their city. Claudio looked a little bemused and I asked him in Italian what was wrong. He turned to me and, with a deadly straight face, asked me, 'Do they not speak English in

Scotland?' The accent had totally confused him along with the speed at which Glaswegians talk.

I roared with laughter as did all my friends when I told them. Claudio saw the funny side of it, too.

Comedian Andy Cameron singled out Claudio that night for some good-hearted 'stick'. I translated again and Claudio had a wonderful night.

Ally Graham – Raith Rovers, Motherwell and Ayr United

It's a wet and windy day at Cliftonhill, Coatbridge, and East Stirling are the visitors taking on the mighty Albion Rovers. The crowd is in the region of two hundred. Celtic legend and Lisbon Lion Tommy Gemmell is the man in charge of Rovers. Big Tam, he of the legendary cannonball shot, is getting a little on the irate side with his team. He is urging his side to close down an East Stirling full-back who has ventured up field. 'Close him! Close him!' the big man bellows. 'Effin close him!'

Still the defender surges forward.

Big Tam turns to me in the dug out and says, 'He's gonnae shoot, he's gonnae effin shoot.'

From 40 yards the defender lets fly.

'He's shot, he's bloody shot. He effin thinks he's ME!'

Brilliant and it reduced me to tears.

Denis Law – Manchester United and Scotland

One of the questions I am asked most often is what was I doing the day England won the World Cup. My answer is always the same and it is absolutely true, I was out on the golf course. Here is the full story of how it came about.

The week before the World Cup Final, I was out playing a round of golf with an English pal of mine. I have to be truly honest here – he hammered me! I said, 'We must have a re-match.' And he replied cockily, 'Anytime!'

I thought 'that will do me'. An hour before the World Cup Final was due to kick off, I turned up at his door and said, 'Anytime, you said. Well now's the time.' 'But Denis, I want to see the game,' he pleaded. 'Tough, the deal was anytime and now is the time.'

We had the course to ourselves and I beat him. When we came in, there were lots of celebrations in the club house but I declined the offer of a drink and headed for home. All I could think of was that, when I went back to the Manchester United dressing room in the new season, I was going to be wound up by Bobby Charlton and Nobby Stiles.

The great thing was Scotland went out and beat England 3–2 at Wembley when they had just been crowned World Champions. It was a quiet dressing room after that.

Donald McLean – Ex-Queen's Park

I played for Queen's Park in the 1950s and 60s and one of my team mates was the present vice president of MDC, Sir Alex Ferguson. I recall an occasion, when we were training at Lesser Hampden, when Alex had a scuffle with a guy called Jimmy Hewlett. Our coach (who I think was Billy Williamson who had played for Rangers) sent the pair of them back to the gym at Hampden to 'put on the gloves' and sort themselves out. Needless to say, by the time they had reached the gym, they had cooled off and both came back to resume our training session, without further rancour!

Another occasion which I recollect was at Perth, home to St Johnstone. The park at that time was Muirton Park (now the home to Asda!). My position in the team was at inside left (now called left midfield). We were attacking, as usual, and I had drifted out to the left wing, on the touchline. The ball was passed to me and as I was looking up before receiving it, to decide which 'defence splitting' pass to make (!), the ball slipped past my outstretched foot and out for a throw-in. Being upset by my carelessness I said (or blasphemed), 'Oh, Christ!' A wag from Perth, standing just behind me on the terracing, shouted back, 'He's no' there to hear you son!' Goodness knows what the response would be from today's fan!

We used to train quite hard on at least three evenings a week. Remember we were amateurs and so had to work or study during the day. Having said that, quite a few of the pros we played were part-time, so they too, only trained in the evening. However, we were well motivated and greatly desired to beat the professionals. We had a captain called Willie Hastie whose last comment to us as we were leaving the locker room to take to the field, was always, 'Remember now, boys, retaliate first!'

In our training sessions we used to run up and down the terracing steps at Hampden – at that time the terracing was twice as high as it is now – so you can imagine how we felt. We used to joke that we could challenge anyone to race up and down steps, but we couldn't win football matches!

Doug Newlands – Ex-Aberdeen and Burnley

In 1951, on collecting one of my first pay packets, in a 'wee brown envelope', containing the then princely sum of £10, Ian Rodger – well known for his thrift – offered me some words of wisdom – 'Don't count the last pound note, Doug – there may be two stuck together. Not much chance there as the team was Aberdeen FC, after all!

In 1958 after a Burnley summer tour to Austria, Czechoslovakia and Poland we were at our last after-match dinner and, bearing in mind the austerity still in these countries at that time, we had VEAL on every previous occasion as a main course. This prompted our fullback, Dave Smith (a Scot) to say – tongue in cheek – 'As a finale, a rendition of Vera Lynn's classic – 'V'e'll Meat Again' would be appropriate'!

In 1957, on a Burnley team coach journey to play Wolves, one of the lads casually asked, 'How far is it to

Wolverhampton?' Our trainer, Ray Bennison, a former Welsh international, looked out of the window and, seeing a signpost replied, in all sincerity, 'It's only A43 miles!' He didn't live that down for quite a few seasons.

In 1957, in a match against Chelsea, Burnley's wing-half, Les Shannon, and their centre forward clashed and ended up entangled in a heap – the outcome being that Les was stretchered off with blood all over his shorts. Not until we reached the dressing room did we realise that Bentley did have the 'bit' between his teeth. Poor Les was left feeling very uncomfortable for a couple of weeks and encased in cotton wool!

Jim McArthur – Hibernian

As you probably know I played for Hibernian FC for 11 years between 1972 and 1983. After I finished playing football, I was at a local football match when a young boy of around 11 years old came up to me and said, 'Hey, mister, ma dad says you used to be Jim McArthur!'

Jimmy Lachlan – St Johnstone

In the late 50s and early 60s, St Johnstone was managed by Bobby Brown who decided in order to wake his team up and prepare them for the game ahead he would get his physio to hand out smelling salts. So before every game each player was handed a small white phial to smell before going on to the pitch.

Unfortunately, a sharp eyed observer spotted this and wrote to the local newspaper with his story, saying that it was no wonder Saints weren't doing very well when they are all going on the pitch smoking!

Mick Worswick – Wigan Athletic

My story involves a mate of mine, Mickey Taylor, who I played with as a semi-pro for Wigan Athletic in the 1973 FA Trophy Final against Scarborough at Wembley.

Some years after Mick's retirement from the semi-pro game, he was playing in a local Summer League match for our village team, Woodplumpton, near Preston, when he collapsed in a heap after a very late tackle on him. The local bobby, Keith Talbot, who doubled up as the team's sponge man, sprinted on to the pitch with his bucket and little bag of tricks and, on reaching the scene of the crime, uttered the following words, 'Mickey, do you want the spray?' to which Mickey immediately replied, 'Why? Is my f***ing hair out of place?' As you can imagine all, the usual bad feeling that comes after a nasty tackle went out of the window as both teams fell about laughing.

Mike Hart – Amateur Footballer from Norwich

When I was younger (much younger) I played for

Wake Green Amateurs in the Birmingham AFA League. I was a very poor goalkeeper and the other players called me Cinderella because I had great difficulty in getting to the ball. In one match I let in 8 goals and afterwards in the dressing room I put my head in my hands and dropped it. On the way home I was so desperate I tried to commit suicide by throwing myself under a bus that rolled under me.

Later on I moved to Norwich and wanted to watch Norwich City. I asked a policeman the way. 'Just follow the crowd,' he said and I ended up at Tesco's.

As you know Norwich have just built a new stand and there have been many complaints from the spectators because it faces the pitch.

When Bruce Rioch came as manager the team were miserable and depressed but he turned it all round – they became depressed and miserable. He swapped the reserves for a lawn mower because he heard it covered more ground.

Nick Harrison – Amateur Footballer

This is a true story from amateur football on Sunday mornings. I was actually there. We had a right fullback who had a reputation for powerful right foot (a right hoofer we called him). Unfortunately, his IQ did not match the power of his kicking and he had a bit of a reputation as a bit of a drinker. I hope you get the picture.

We were getting ready for the match. The banter going round the changing room was livelier than usual as we were confident of an easy win. The conversation switched to what the activities had been the night before. A player next to me said he came in from the pub, put the TV on and ended up watching *Rita, Sue and Bob Too*. This started a snowball of input from different quarters, relaying their funniest bits from the film. I noticed our 'hoofer' of a fullback was not participating at all. As the conversation slowly ceased, I asked the hoofer, 'Eh, Stocksy, have you seen *Rita, Sue and Bob Too*?'

He replied, in total seriousness, 'No, mate, I haven't even seen the first one.'

The players around us just collapsed. Of course all the other players wanted to know what the story was and as the tale was repeated over and over the whole changing room ended up in tears.

PS We won the game – after extra time!

Steve Corbett – Innsworth Youth Club Player

I used to play for a youth club team in Gloucester – Innsworth YC. We were essentially an under 13 side playing in an under 15 league so, most weeks, we got thumped – in 10 of our defeats, for example, we conceded at least double figures (21–0 was the record). In the league cup, we got through the first round by obtaining a bye, only to meet our match in the next round, losing 19–1. Anyway, at that time, like many youngsters, I kept a diary. One genuine entry for Saturday March 2nd 1968 recorded two completely unconnected events: 'Morning – played against 66 Starr Youth Club. Lost 20–0. Afternoon – went to optician's.'

My footballing career progressed at Plymouth Polytechnic where we had some useful keepers. Dave, the first-eleven goalie, was a former county youth player and, as was the fashion at the time, was known as 'The Cat', after Chelsea's Peter Bonetti. Over the years Alan and Kevin shared the second-eleven jersey. Alan's surname was Jacobs so he was called 'Crackers' while Kevin was occasionally called Teflon (non-stick?). The third-team keeper, Keith, was actually quite decent but being rather short-sighted played in a pair of heavy rimmed spectacles. In a variation of The Cat, he was known as 'The Bat' (as in, blind as a —)

I seem to recall that around this time the French national side occasionally fielded a keeper whose genuine surname was Dropsy.

Tim Branagh – Amateur Footballer

While playing for an Amateur League team in the 1990s in Northern Ireland, we appointed an ex-Irish League semi-professional 'star' as manager. Keen to whip us junior boys into shape, he would give very aggressive lectures to us, detailing what he expected from us prior to every match. On one famous occasion and while in full flow, he demanded that our 'front two close down the baldy haired centre-half as soon as he got the ball!' Oh boy did he get reminded of this slip over the following years.

5

MANAGERS

Alan Curbishley – Charlton Athletic

After an away win and on the bus back home, the talk was loud and lively. A few of the players were talking about what they were going to do that evening and the conversation got round to eating out. Scott Parker had just broken into the first-team squad and was a little shy about joining in.

The players were talking about their favourite foods and restaurants and Scott decided to join in by saying that his favourite food was Chinese and that he would be going for a Chinese meal with his girlfriend that evening.

The conversation then got onto their favourite dishes and Scott, now feeling part of the team stated, 'Oh, it's all great! I like the sizzling dishes, noodles and rice but what I really like most is the ANIMATED DUCK with pancakes!'

Alex McLeish – Rangers

On a European visit with the Aberdeen FC team, Gordon Strachan and I shared a room with our big centre-half, Willie Garner, who talked in his sleep. Gordon awoke one night to find Willie stroking his holdall and calling it a 'good dog'. Wee Gordon was alarmed and asked Willie what he was doing. Willie, in sleep-walk mode, turned on Gordon aggressively and cornered him. Gordon, quick as a flash, diffused the situation by saying, 'Do you want me to take your Adidas bag for a walk?'

Billy Stark – Queen's Park

This is a true story from my time at Aberdeen under Sir Alex Ferguson.

Injured players, after treatment, would go through to the multi-gym where there was also a snooker table. Obviously snooker was out when you were supposed to be working back to fitness. However, one day, two young injured lads decided to have a game of snooker whilst the boss and players were at training.

Anyway, Sir Alex happened to still be in the building and was always identifiable by a little cough which the players duly heard coming along the corridor. At that point, one of the players dived on to the multi-gym leaving the other isolated at the far end, snooker cue in hand. When Sir Alex came in and caught them, the young lad panicked and proceeded to pretend he was doing exercises with the snooker cue!

Craig Brown – Ex-Scotland

Rangers were playing Ajax in a Champions League away match. Ally McCoist was unfit and did not make the journey. Instead he was invited to be part of the commentary team for the television coverage. That morning he was in the treatment room at Ibrox with three of the Rangers apprentices. They were surprised to see him there, having expected him to travel with the team even if he was not playing.

'I'm going to be seeing the game at the television studio,' Ally told them. 'I'm an expert and I'll be giving my opinions. If you look in tonight, you'll see me on the screen.'

One of the lads asked him what he would say. 'That depends on the match,' said Ally, who then decided to have a bit of fun with these young lads. 'Why? What do you want me to say?'

They laughed but Ally pressed them and told them to pick something for him to say and then go to the pub to watch the TV and make a few pounds by betting on him coming out with those words. The lads decided to take him up on it and one of them, seeing a pools coupon in the room, said, 'There's one for you, Ally – say the word coupon.'

'That's not really about football,' protested Ally but the lad insisted.

A second one looked at the diagram of a human body on the wall and told McCoist he must use the word tibia. Not to be outdone, the third one picked the word piriformis, which is a muscle around the backside. Ally squirmed a little but the lads jibed that he had boasted he could say anything on television so he decided to do his best. He insisted that the boy write piriformis down on a piece of paper which he tore from the *Daily Record* – or the *Daily Ranger*, as he likes to call it. Later, in the studio, the presenter, Dougie Donnelly, asked him how he thought the game would go.

'Well, this is going tibia difficult game for Rangers but, if we win, it will be a real coupon-buster,' said Ally, delighted that he had already managed to squeeze in two of his designated words. The third word was a real struggle, however. Eventually, about halfway through the first half, Rangers were two goals down, Paul Gascoigne had been ordered off and there was an air of depression around the studio. He was asked for a comment and Ally as usual had the perfect response, 'This is the worst Rangers piriformis I've seen all season!'

Bob Shankly hated players to be unfit or injured. When they were injured, the players would very often be snubbed – ignored until they were fit again.

There was a guy called Rab Duffin, a very good inside forward who played for Stirling. He had been out for some time with a shoulder injury and, during one particular evening training session at Annfield, Stirling's ground before they moved to their plush new stadium, there were a number of players participating. Bob Shankly saw Rab Duffin pressing himself against a wall. The player was embarrassed at the general manager seeing him not training with the other players but having his own work-out. Bob grunted something, which was his way if he came across a player not training to the full because of a fitness problem. 'I'm doing exercises, boss,' Rab said, not wishing to appear to be taking it easy.

Shankly replied with another grind of apparent disapproval.

Rab tried his best and continued, 'In fact, I feel like Christ.' This was a reference to his exercise, in which his arms and legs were outstretched against the wall.

Shankly's response was both quick and clear. 'Well, son, you might feel like Christ, you might even look like Christ but Christ was back with us in three days – you've been out for six weeks!'

One of my favourite stories concerns the time when there was a problem with mice at Dundee. Mousetraps proved to be useless so Lawrie Smith, our physio, was sent to get a cat. Sure enough the cat took up residence and did a fine job devastating the Dundee mouse population.

However, the cat was a bit lazy and used to love to curl up in the boot room where it was always warm. One morning, Alex Hamilton came in early – probably because he had not been home from the night before. He went to the boot room and there was the cat snoring across his boots. Very gently Alex put his toe under the cat and flicked it a little way into the air so that it landed safely on all four feet. He did not realise that Bob Shankly was standing in the doorway behind him. 'Hammy,' said Shankly, 'when you've done as much for his club as that cat, then you can put your boot behind him!' As you can see, Shankly's reputation for bluntness and wit was not without foundation.

Talking of Bob Shankly, he had a way of elevating his players to the opposition while keeping them humble within their own company. Just to give you an example, at the start of one of my seasons at Dundee, we were having the usual team photograph taken and Bob was organising where everyone was to be in the photo. If you had not re-signed for the season, then you could not be in the photo at all. Those that were in could tell how they stood in the manager's estimation by where he positioned them. If you were in the middle you knew that you were in good standing with the manager.

I can remember Doug Huston and I were waiting and waiting while he gave thought to where he wanted everyone. Fortunately, we were among those placed early on. It was usually the young lads were left until last, and Bob would have them positioned at the very ends of the rows with such encouraging words as, 'A pair of scissors'll get rid of you two.'

Dario Grady – Crewe Alexandra

Many years ago when I was manager of Wimbledon Football Club, we were playing away at Aldershot, both of us in the old Fourth Division. Just before we went out to play, there was a knock on the dressing room door. 'Who is it?' I asked.

'Tommy McAnearney,' came the reply from their manager.

Quick as a flash one of my players said, 'Come in, the three of you!'

David Moyes – Everton

I always remember playing for Bristol City against Derby County at Ashton Gate. We had a winger called Howard Pritchard and he was up against John Gregory and they were having a rare old tussle. Anyway, at one point they both slid in for a fifty-fifty challenge and the momentum carried them both over the touchline and they ended up by the dugouts.

John obviously wasn't happy with the challenge and the first thing he could lay his hands on was the trainer's bucket of water. He was really riled and so he picked up the bucket and hurled the water all over Howard! I couldn't believe it and Howard was absolutely saturated but, as if that wasn't bad enough, the referee just let it pass! John wasn't booked or anything and yet poor Howard was drenched.

Dennis Booth – Carlisle

I was playing for Lincoln City with Graham Taylor as my manager. We were just going out of the dressing room to start an FA cup match against Burnley and Graham was standing on the benches giving us some final words of encouragement when he came out with, 'Don't shight fy of anything.' He wondered why we all had to troop back in to regroup!

I was playing for Southend managed by Arthur Rowley. We were 2–0 down at half time. Arthur was berating our full back regarding the opposition winger, as both goals had come from crosses from the winger. The full back was adamant that no one was crossing from his side of the pitch. The argument died down and, just as we were going out for the second half, Arthur said, 'Just a minute – somebody had better pick up the linesman then because somebody is crossing that ball!'

Jim Leishman – Dunfermline Athletic

'I was the first professional football player to be forced to retire due to public demand.'

Jim Moffat – East Fife

It was rumoured that there was conflict in a team's dressing room between players deciding on a nick-name for their goalkeeper. Some wanted Cinderella because he kept missing the ball, while others pre-ferred Dracula because he was terrified of crosses.

Making his way to training one morning, a young pro-fessional goalkeeper's curiosity was aroused when he heard screaming and shouting from a nearby street. As he turned into the street, he could see that a block of flats was on fire and trapped on the upper storey was a woman frantically clutching her baby boy. The small crowd of people who had gathered below her were try-ing unsuccessfully to persuade her to release the boy into their waiting arms. On arrival at the scene, the young goalkeeper then pleaded with the woman to throw her child to him reassuring her that he was the local football team's goalkeeper so she needn't worry about him dropping the baby. Feeling safer with this knowledge she finally relented and released her boy. The young goalkeeper caught the falling child superbly but then proceeded to bounce him twice off the ground before kicking him a full 50 yards up the street.

It's sometimes quite fascinating to realise how many people from varying walks of life share the same name e.g. Mike Reid (former Radio 1 DJ) and Mike Reid (actor), Jim McLean (sports writer) and Jim McLean (former Dundee Utd chairman and manager) and John Williams (guitarist) and John Williams (former Welsh Rugby Union internationalist). Veteran goalkeeper Ray Charles, once capped for Scotland at 'B' International level, is no exception. He, of course, shares his name with that great American blues singer-songwriter Ray Charles. The similarities, however, stop at their names. The main difference being that Ray Charles the singer-songwriter is blind. While having every respect for the unfortunate American, it does put a new perspective on the match report seen in a Sunday newspaper in the 80s where the journalist reported that 'the Airdrie striker put the game beyond doubt when he slammed the ball past the UNSIGHTED Ray Charles in the East Fife goal'.

Joe Royle – Ipswich Town

Many years ago when I was a player at Oldham, I returned back from training with Coach Bill Urnsom to find all the lights turned off in the main lounge. Bill started muttering and cursing about keeping the lights off for economical reasons. We then both burst into the lounge to find a grieving family ready to spread their father's ashes on to the pitch. Billy's face on meeting the family lit up the room with embarrassment and he then spent the next five minutes apologising for his blasphemous outburst.

John Connolly – Queen of the South and Ex-St Johnstone

In 1970 the St Johnstone manager, Willie Ormond, was giving a pre-match talk using a tactics board. Willie picked up a player disc from the board and said, 'He's hopeless.' He then picked another player from the board and said, 'He's hopeless.' Then he picked a third player from the board and said, 'He's hopeless.'

Willie then turned to the team and said, 'And, if you can't beat a side with eight men, then you are all hopeless!'

John Lambie – Ex-Partick Thistle

It's a cold night in the north-west of Glasgow. The

mighty Thistle are at home to Hibs and it turns out to be not such a good night for Jags striker Colin McGlashan.

McGlashan rises for a high ball with a Hibs defender and ends up in a heap on the ground. The magic sponge, for once, fails to work and the late John Hart shouts to the dugout and me, 'He's badly concussed boss – he doesn't even know who he is.'

Without a pause, I answer, 'He disnae know who he is? Tell him he's effin' Pele and get him back out there.'

Ray Lewington – Ex-Watford

We were playing at home and drawing 0–0 in what was a dreadful match. The manager had come down to the dugout midway through the first half to make a substitution. The crowd had given him some verbal abuse on his way down and you could tell he was agitated.

'Get the numbers, Bamber,' he grumbled to the physio. ('Bamber' was the nickname of our physiotherapist, who looked uncannily like Bamber Gasgoine of *University Challenge* fame, even down to the round rimmed glasses.) The manager and 'Bamber' disliked each other primarily because the manager thought, as they did in these days, that he should have the final say as to what players could play and train and that 'Bamber', being only a qualified physiotherapist, did not!

'What number?' asked Bamber.

'All of them' answered the manager.

'What number?' queried Bamber again.

'I said bring f***ing all of them – I haven't decided yet!' barked the manager.

After five minutes, the manager decided to bring off one of the strikers, a player who liked to wear the No 7 shirt (remember this was before the days of squad numbers), but, on this occasion, he was wearing the No 10 shirt. No 7 was being worn (unfortunately for the manager) by the only player having a half-decent game for us, on the right wing.

6

REFEREES

Cliff Brooks – North Wales Coast

During my time refereeing, I enjoyed the changing facilities! Having changed in a railway goods van, an air-raid shelter, a mental hospital ward, the lounge bar of a pub and sometimes in my own car, the facilities at Rhyl, where I could even have a nice hot bath after a mucky game, were a welcome sight.

I remember a linesman at Sealand being particularly annoyed at one of my decisions in a North Wales Coast Junior Cup Tie. He charged on to the field, slung the flag at me and told me, in no uncertain terms, what he thought. Book in hand, I enquired of his name.

'Donald Duck' he replied.

After the match, he apologised and gave me his name but, as I said in my report, it must have been the first time Donald Duck was reported for such ungentlemanly conduct! I am sure the Coast FA secretary thought I was 'quackers'!

On another occasion I was at a Welsh League game at Bethesda where I was regularly threatened that I would be thrown in the nearby river. On this occasion, for some unknown reason, neither the linesman nor I had brought flags. We obtained one flag from the away team, Blaenau, but, when looking for something else suitable, we found a box full of jumble from a sale held in aid of club funds. In the box we found a pair of ladies' bloomers – the type with the elastic at the knee! – and yes THEY became the second flag – 'Converted Bloomers'! It was one occasion when a linesman did make a bloomer!

Dave Edmundson

For many years I was a PE teacher in charge of sport at a large private school in Blackburn and I refereed school matches on many occasions. Two incidents spring to mind.

The first involved our 1st XI goalkeeper. The ball went out for a goal kick and I turned my back to run back towards the centre of the field to await the long clearance upfield. Suddenly there was a shout and I turned round to see the opposing centre forward following the ball into our net. I awarded the goal thinking the goalie had miscued and just sent it straight to the opposition's No 9. As we lined up for the re start, I was disconcerted when the some of the other team members asked me repeatedly if the goal would count. I knew then I may not have perceived the correct outcome.

What had happened is that our keeper had quickly tried to take a short goal kick across the area to his full back who had dropped off but had actually kicked the ball into his own net! How? I shall never know

I let the goal stand – a totally wrong decision – and suffered some embarrassment as a result but not half as much as our goalkeeper.

Another refereeing incident occurred when I was officiating on a Saturday afternoon for the Old Boys. This was in the Lancashire Amateur League. In schoolboy football, I never concerned myself with red/yellow cards or even official 'bookings'. A schoolmaster's authority was enough. But, in a properly constituted league, I had to ensure that things were properly documented. I only ever booked one person. And even then I probably let things go on a little too long. My patience finally ran out and I called the offender over. 'I'm booking you for persistent backchat and abuse of the match officials. What is your name?'

'Dave Edmundson,' was the reply.

Taken aback, I thought this was a continuation of his attitude. 'Do you want me to send you off?' I said. 'I'll ask you once more. What is your name?'

'Honest, ref, it's Dave Edmundson.'

This was then confirmed by a team mate.

So, in 23 years of refereeing, I only booked and took the name of one player. And that name, by a huge quirk of coincidence, was my own!

David Elleray – Premiership

Of all the rogues I refereed the two I enjoyed being on the field with most were Dennis Wise and Robbie Savage. Dennis was totally unpredictable on and off the field as I discovered when he gave me a pre-match kiss in the tunnel at Anfield. He always had an opinion on everything and many of our encounters became 'Den and Dave' conversations.

Chelsea played Nottingham Forest in a League Cup tie and there was a scuffle between two players. I decided that a lecture would suffice but, no sooner had I started, than Dennis (who had not been involved) butted in and said, 'Just send the f*****s off, David!' We all burst out laughing and he had done my job for me.

A while later, I noticed that he had a bruise on his nose and, jokingly, I asked if someone had hit him. 'Yeah, me old lady!'

There were times when I could cheerfully have given him a good smack but referees are not allowed to do that, at least not intentionally. However, Robbie Savage was on the receiving end of referee Matt Messias's elbow at Newcastle when Messias signalled for a free-kick and caught Savage in the face and knocked him out. It was something many referees would love to have done and Alan Shearer helped relieve the tension by showing Messias the red card. It was one of the highlights of the season for many people!

Douglas Harrison – Birmingham District League

In the Birmingham League I dreaded refereeing a particular Community Association side because of a certain centre forward who I will call 'Stuttering Charlie' – not unkindly said because he did stutter badly and his name was Charlie! The classic came when he was brought down in the penalty area but nevertheless managed to score a goal which he was pleased with but then he demanded the penalty as well!

The whole field and all the spectators were hysterical as he shouted at me, 'You c-c-c-call yourself a referee? You know n-n-nothing about f-f-f-football!

I was too hysterical to book him but he hated me even more in future games.

In 1960 I left my school for one year to go on further training. I came back to a team I had nurtured but had also penalised for any misdemeanour. In the first match, the first five minutes went well and then, to my horror, the centre-forward shouted to his outside right, 'Pass the ball, Arse!'

I stopped the game and said, 'You are off if there is any more of that.' Then it happened again with another but I left it until half-time.

The captain came up and said, 'We have realised what the trouble is, Mr Harrison. A new boy joined the club while you were away. His name is BUMFITT.'

George Clyde

I was a referee on the Grade 1 list for 14 seasons and only retired this year. One of the funniest moments was at a match between Cowdenbeath and Stenhousemuir involving the character Terry Christie who was the manager of Stenhousemuir. He is renowned in football circles for verbally battering referees – being a head-master it was always polite but you got the drift of what he was saying! During the game, he continually gave me pelters for not giving his team fouls but instead playing advantage. After half-time, he leapt from the technical area screaming for a penalty but no one else on the bench moved. I had a wee laugh and reminded him that we had turned round at half time and this was, in fact, now his own penalty area. He gave his own technical staff a battering for not reminding him and letting me get my own back.

John Rowbotham – Scottish Premiership

I was asked to appear in the making of the film *A Shot at Glory*. The final scenes were to be filmed at Hamp-den Park between Kilnockie and Rangers. Before set-ting off, I thought I'd better get the old dome looking its best. So I rubbed on my best shining gel and set off for Hampden. On my arrival, I was taken down to make-up and sat in front of the mirror. 'Looking good,' I thought. Just then, the make-up lady took out a small pad and started to dab my head. 'What are you doing?' I asked.

'Your head's too shiny – the glare would be too much for the camera so I'm dulling it down', she replied.

Later on, during a break in the filming, there was, from a section of the crowd, containing 'extras' from the film a song. To the tune of 'Dixie' came the words, 'John Rowbotham you're a horse's A R S E, doo-dah, doodah!'

When I looked up, I saw four guys standing up with the aforementioned letters stamped on their chest. They were the 'extra' fans who had the letters of R A N G E R S stamped on their chests and had been filmed standing cheering on their team. Four of them had changed seats and, as they sang their song, stood up to reveal their opinion of me.

I thought it was hilarious. (SO DID EVERYONE ELSE AT HAMPDEN!)

Mike Dimblebee – English Football League 1977–88

The date of the incident is Saturday 29 October 1980 and it concerns the 3rd Division game between Swindon Town and Hull City. Important to the story – this game marked the League debut of 16-year-old Paul Rideout, later to become a much-travelled English international and who was later, I believe, to play for, among many other clubs, Rangers. The other important player in the piece was Chris Kamara, the then Swindon captain, who was (in my opinion) one of the finest journeymen professionals of his day. He (Kamara) always seemed to be the captain of his side wherever he played and again, in my opinion, set a wonderful example to his team mates as a great leader of his team. Most surprisingly he did not make much of an impact as a manager but has I believe gone on to be a respected analyst for Sky Sport.

Anyway, as the game proceeded, on several occasions, as was his wont, Kamara had a friendly banter with myself. Such things as, 'Our ball, Referee!', 'Offside, Referee!', 'Corner kick, Referee!' and the myriad of comments that occur in all games. These were usually personal comments to me and I could cope with all of these and responded, or more often didn't, as was necessary at the time. Kamara always made these comments while getting on with his own game in a hard and competitive, yet fair, way. He always knew when and where to toe the line and was a pleasure for me to referee him.

We now come to the crux of the story. After about 20 minutes, with the score 0–0, Rideout (on his debut, remember) comes on to the ball about 40 yards from goal along an 'inside left channel', dribbles about 10 yards and then hits an unstoppable shot that rockets into the top left-hand corner of the net. The Swindon players turn to congratulate the jubilant young debutante while I spot the linesman (as they were called in those days!) flagging for offside against a player somewhere near the penalty spot. I immediately award a free kick to Hull which is taken before most of the players and spectators realise what has happened. On recovering his position and wanting an explanation, Kamara eventually gets close enough to speak to me. All this time you must realise that the game is proceeding and it takes a few minutes for all this to happen. 'May I speak to you, Mr Dimblebee?' says Kamara. 'You usually do' says I ... play still proceeding ...'I believe you to be the best Referee on the list, Mr Dimblebee – but that was the worst decision I have seen in my life' says Kamara when we next meet. So what do I do? Remember the exchange of words were personal between Kamara and myself and not heard by others. I like to believe that Kamara was being genuine with his comments about me being (in his opinion) 'the best on the list' and I am equally certain that at that time he did think it to be 'the worst decision he had ever seen'. Needless to say I took no action against Chris Kamara, apart from a big smile to myself and the verbal exchanges remained between ourselves.

At the completion of the game Kamara, as ever with him, was one of the first to thank me and we smiled about the incident. His attitude as a Captain was always exemplary and it is a sad reflection on the game that the rapport that there was generally between players and officials does not exist today. Finally to complete the story, Swindon won a keenly fought game 3-1 and the young Rideout did later score a good goal to mark his debut – but not the great one he might have done.

Mike Riley – Premiership

Hill 16 is probably the most famous sloping pitch in Rotherham, perched on the side of Herringthorpe playing fields, with a slope of about six feet from one end to the other. And for me it is the scene of my most embarrassing moments as a referee. One freezing January morning, I was refereeing an entertaining match where the players were doing their best to ignore the heavy mud, lashing rain and strong winds. As I set off to chase an attack, I clipped my heel against a player, tripped and set off head-first into a swallow dive. Going downhill I skated about 30 yards before coming to a stop in a rather large puddle. I was covered from head to foot in very cold, clinging mud. Ever the professional, my first thought was to stop the game, so I jumped to my feet and tried to blow my whistle. The mouthful of mud tasted so nice and all that came out of the whistle was a spray of muddy water. I shouldn't have worried though because, as I looked around, the game had already stopped. All the players were bent-double, killing themselves laughing.

7

FANS

**Alan Noble – Vice President of
the Muscular Dystrophy Campaign**

THE RISING COSTS OF (A) FOOTBALL
Some years ago I decided to assemble a complete collection of autographed footballs of the Scottish Clubs
of the day – twelve in total. I did this with the help of
Wallace Mercer who was Chairman of Heart of Mid-
lothian at that time (he furnished me with all the contact names at the various clubs). The idea was to raise
money for the Muscular Dystrophy Group

All was going well – very well – in fact, the clubs not
only sent an autographed football, but also a club scarf
and pennant. My presentation cabinet was looking
absolutely fabulous except for one thing – I had
received nothing from Clydebank FC. I took the bull by
the horns and telephoned the boss, Jack Steedman. I
explained that my collection was complete except for
Clydebank – he was very polite and most understand-
ing and I quote what he said, 'I think what you are
doing is most credible, and for such a worthy cause,
but have you ever stopped to consider the cost of one

of these footballs. Would you not rather have a couple of players instead?'

All turned out OK – Mr Steedman did forward an autographed Clydebank FC football, along with a scarf and pennant – my collection was complete and it raised £1000 for the charity appeal.

Alan Ogden – Leeds Fan

John Charles was walking through the centre of Leeds one afternoon when a man came up to him and said, 'Hello, John, remember me?'

John was rather taken aback. 'I'm sorry, I don't,' he replied.

'Well,' said the man, 'do you remember a game at Elland Road, the score was one goal apiece and you took a penalty ten minutes from full-time? You blasted the ball over the bar into the crowd. I was the guy who threw it back to you.'

Alan Smith (team unknown)

This story involves Bill Shankly.

Bill Shankly was being interviewed by a young television reporter who asked Bill to name his greatest 11 of all time. Eventually they reached the forward-line and the young man enquired, 'What about Tom Finney, would he get into your team?' In a heartbeat (as they say in the States) he replied, 'Wearing a raincoat, son!' Little did the interviewer know that Shanks thought 'Tommy' (as he always referred to him) was the greatest footballer to walk this Earth.

This second story involves me and my two sons, now 29 and 32.

The younger boy was nine years only and making his debut with the local team (ages varied from 9 – 16) and naturally I went to support them. The opposition, local rivals, had a boy playing who was about 13, tall and very uncoordinated. He kicked the opposition more than he kicked the ball. I was beside myself as, miraculously, he avoided maiming his opponents, until he caught my elder boy with a very clumsy tackle. My son let out a shriek and fell to the ground clutching his leg, which I thought, at best, would be broken. I remonstrated with the referee and entered the field of play, confronting the referee with the immortal words, 'THAT'S MY LAD OUT THERE!' To this day I'm still taunted whenever and wherever they all meet.

Alistair Meldrum – St Johnstone Fan

Where I work there is a strong interest in football and each Monday the conversation revolves around the fortunes of the various teams, Tottenham, Arsenal, Chelsea, Liverpool and Man U. However each Monday the conversation stopper is my voice chiming in with, 'St Johnsone did . . .'!

Andy Brown – Fulham Fan

The strangest occurrence regarding a football match happened on a holiday to Majorca when I was in my early twenties.

During a night in the hotel bar a couple of us were persuaded, by a guy who was there with his two sons, to turn out for a 'tourist' 11 against the hotel staff 11. The morning of the match arrived and the staff had begged a pitch from the local club. Both teams turned out in whatever kit they could find. The one man to be fully kitted out was the referee – the guy who had got us all to play. The match was a one-sided affair with our 12 against their 11 and the ref constantly blowing whenever his sons got tackled. We ended up winning 4–2 having been given two dodgy penalties. It turned out that he took his ref's kit on every holiday much to the embarrassment of his two sons, who were too frightened to tell him to leave it at home.

Andy Obarski – Hearts Fan

Although I have lived in Jersey for many years I am a Fifer born and bred and a long time Hearts supporter, which is a bit of a joke in itself! I have recalled a sort of amusing joke which is loosely football related.

The Lone Ranger and Tonto are in Glasgow on vacation when a ghastly murder is committed. The local gendarmerie are baffled and ask the fabled duo if they could be of some assistance in tracking down the murderer. Only too happy to aid Anglo–American relations they agree to look at the facts. The first thing they ask to see is the murder weapon which turns out to be a six-inch arrow with green feathers. Immediately Tonto turns to the chief inspector and informs him that the perpetrator was definitely a Celtic supporter.

'But how can you tell that, Tonto?' he enquired.

'It's easy, white man,' replied Tonto, 'Wee arra people.'

Boom, boom.

When Bob Paisley signed Avi Cohen in 1979, he received a telephone call from Alex Ferguson (prior to his 'Sir' days). The gist of the call went along the following lines:

AF 'Bob, do you realise that the lad Cohen is Jewish?'
BP 'Of course I do Alex but what difference does the boy's religion make?'
AF 'Well, Bob, you have to realise that he cannae play on a Saturday.'
BP 'Ach, Alex, don't bother yourself, I've got another five or six of them already!'

Anthony Saddler – Manchester City Fan

Years ago (35 approx.), I was housemaster at a London school. Being keen on (a) football and (b) winning football matches, I liked my house to do well in the knock-out comp each year. One year, we reached the final with a good team and a favourite's chance of taking the trophy. However, we had reckoned without the cunning tactics of our opponents who, to nullify any effect I might have on the touchline, deployed their whole house to either side of me and, every time I shouted either encouragement or tactical advice, they drowned my voice with their own chorus of 'Come on'. Puts a whole different meaning to the concept of 'man-marking'! Amusingly, I cannot remember the result but I do recall the incident which has always made me smile.

Arthur Critchley – Bolton Wanderers Fan

A couple of years ago I helped to supervise a football tour of Holland by a team of 14–15-year-old boys from St Helens, Merseyside. They did not like the food in the hotel and one evening declared, 'We don't like this foreign muck – we want some good English food. We are going out for a pizza!'

Bill Fairweather – St Johnstone Fan

As a very long-suffering Saints supporter (dating back well over 50 years!), I may have many sad stories –

which I have been trying to forget! – but my one real gem goes back a long way to the Willie Peat era at the end of the 1940s.

He was a wee bit 'long in the tooth' by the time he came to Saints but was still a good winger. One day, he was having a real 'stinker' and looked like he had his boots on the wrong feet. He was unfortunately 'performing' in front of the stand – there was only one stand in those days, of course and, after a terrible first half, he was going from bad to worse in the second half. At a throw-in, he completely missed the ball, which was too much for a bloke sitting behind me. 'Hey, Willie,' he said, 'that's bloody awful. Come up here and look at yersel'!'

Bob Tindall (team unknown)

Many years ago England had an amateur international team as well as a professional one. The manager of the amateurs was quite a well known FA figure – FNS (Norman) Creek. I am told that, in the dressing room, before an international match against Iceland, Norman enjoined the players, 'I don't want to hear you shouting for the ball because these Icelanders speak very good English!'

Another dressing room story, this time attributed to the late, much-loved Dave Magnall of Queen's Park Rangers who said, 'No fancy stuff now! Bang it down the middle and let them fight for it!'

Brian Heaney – Celtic Fan

We were at Ibrox watching an Old Firm game and Celtic won (I think) 4-1. On that day, there were two Smiths in the Rangers team – Alex and Gordon. Bobby Lennox had had a great game and maybe scored a hat trick. As we were leaving, a big guy (who had obviously had a couple of sherbets) put his arm round me a said, 'What a result, wee man! They might have the Smiths, but we've got the Golden Wonder!'

Many years ago at Firhill, the lines were marked with sawdust and most players had long hair. Thistle had a winger, I'm sure that his surname was Cowan and he was very quick. Flying down the wing, he was tackled by a Celtic defender and rolled out of the playing area, picking up some of the sawdust. Ruffling his hair to remove the sawdust, a wag from the terracing shouted, 'Hey, Cowan, your heid's cracked open.'

Here's another. A journalist friend was in Spain with the Rangers to report on one of the Cup Winners Cup ties. On the way to the match, he was recognised by a fan who enquired, 'Will ye be phonin hame the night?' 'Yes,' he replied. 'Gonnae dae us a favour, pal, an tell the people back hame that Callela has fell?'

Bryan Booth – Middlesbrough Fan

In the days when Jack Charlton managed Middlesbrough, some of the football they served up was so dour that Tommy Docherty once commented that he would rather spend a Saturday afternoon in the dentist's chair than watch 'Boro. This sort of performance was being played out on a cold winter's Saturday and, when one of the opposition went down injured, it seemed to take ages for the trainer to get the player back on his feet whilst the others just stood around waiting in the cold. Eventually, a long-suffering home supporter at the rear of the terraces bellowed, 'For Christ's sake, 'Boro, don't just stand there – PRACTISE'.

At another 'Boro home match, the quality of play was again pathetic. The visitors were winning 1–0 with about five minutes to go to the final whistle. The official came out and displayed No.11 on his board to indicate a substitution by the 'Boro. 'Thank God,' shouted one disgruntled fan, 'they're taking the whole team off.'

In late 1966, 'Boro signed a goalkeeper from Falkirk named Willie Whigham. In one of his early appearances for his new club, I learned from a fan that, when Willie had originally signed for Falkirk, he had been a prolific centre forward and the reason he had become a goalie was that, whenever he scored, none of his team mates would kiss him because he was so ugly!

Clive Maxwell – Bristol Rovers Fan

My family is originally from Skye but moved down to

a much warmer Weston-Super-Mare where our nearest local league team is Bristol Rovers – we don't mention City as they are far too successful.

With my great buddy Mario Ferrari and our dads, we attended in the early 70s a Bristol Rovers home game against Plymouth Argyle on a very, very cold Boxing Day at the old Eastville stadium. Ten or so minutes into the game, Frankie Prince linked up with Harold Jarman who put in a good shot that was athletically saved by the Plymouth goalie who, because of the weather, was wearing black tracksuit bottoms tucked inside his knee high socks.

After an appreciative outbreak of applause from around the ground for a good bit of football, our attention was drawn to the middle-aged couple in front of us who were dressed appropriately in his-and-hers bobble hats and matching Rovers accessories. In a very broad Bristolian accent she was heard to say, 'Yer, my luv, duns't 'e think that Plymouth goalie do look like that there Rudolf Newrayeff?'

He replied, 'I dun' know about that, my lover, 'e do look more like a bloody ballet dancer to I.'

Colin Rawlinson – Bristol Rovers Fan

Len Shackleton of Sunderland was a real character. As most people know, he was always known as the clown prince of football. He was a very skilful player and was known, on more than one occasion, to dispossess a goalkeeper and fly past him, leaving him floundering. Len would dribble past him and then stop just in front of the open goal and shout to the hapless keeper, 'Quick, I haven't scored yet!'

When Jackie Charlton was manager of Middlesbrough, they played very defensively on the basis that, if you didn't concede any goals, you can't be beaten. Unfortunately, the efforts in pursuing this policy gave them little opportunity to score themselves. As a result, the fans changed the club competition from 'Goal of the Month' to 'Month of the Goal'.

Colin Salt – St Albans City Fan

I recall an incident just after the war, either 1946 or 1947, watching a City game from behind the goal at the York Road end. I cannot remember who the opponents were but one of their forwards struck a tremendous hard low shot which beat Bert Rolph, the City keeper all ends up. In those days, the net was secured at the back of the goal to a board, about 18 inches high. The shot struck the board and rebounded straight at Bert who caught it and booted it up field in one swift movement. The ref and linesman never saw it and play continued. The 'goal scorer' was incensed as you can imagine but we local lads thought it a huge joke.

Colin Weir (team unknown)

I played in goal for Oxford University from 1945 to 1948 and in December 1947 we travelled to Dublin to play the Bohemians at Delymount Park. Fog, which had been threatening all day, descended on the ground during the second half of the match when we were leading 3–1. Out of the fog there loomed a Bohemian forward who scored to make the score 3–2 to us. It was in the days when club linesmen ran the line and a reserve from O.U. was doing the job. Suddenly he appeared at my side and informed me that we had already played 55 minutes of the second half. I told him to go and find the referee in the fog and get him to blow the final whistle.

For the next 10 minutes I neither saw nor heard much until, after a second half lasting 65 minutes, the whistle for full-time was blown. As we were leaving the field, I asked the referee why we had played for so long. I said that I thought that this was a friendly match and NOT a cup-tie with extra time. He looked back at me and smilingly remarked, 'Well, we thought we'd try and beat you!'

Craig Findlater – Everton Fan

I'm an Everton fan who lives in Southampton and I teach 11–16-year-olds. Can't take any credit from this as it came from Lawrie McMenemy at a school presentation evening! Lawrie was in New Zealand with the England squad as part of the managerial set-up. Paul Gascoigne was there and in his prime. Every morning Gazza used to come down and order his breakfast prior to training. The order was the same every morning 'Full English, pet, nae mushrooms but plenty of beans.' On the fourth morning, the little Maori waitress says to Gazza, 'I'm really sorry, sir, but you can't have the full English this morning.' 'And why's that, pet?' says Paul. 'Well, sir, I'm afraid we've run out of bacon!' Gazza looks at Lawrie and says, 'Gaffer, can you credit that – nae bacon and all them sheep runnin' aboot in this place!'

Dave Burgess – Fulham Fan

I saw Johnny Haynes make his debut for Fulham at the age of 17 (at Craven Cottage). Haynes was an inside left (No 10) and the left winger (No 11) was Charlie Mitten, an experienced player nearing the end of his career. During the game, Haynes made a beautiful pass to the wing but Mitten didn't get to it. 'Charlee!' exclaimed Haynes with a look of exasperation and hands on hips.

Charlie glared back whereupon a wag in the crowd shouted, 'Smack his arse, Charlie!'

Dave Schofield – Leeds United Fan

THERE'S ALWAYS A KEVIN
When I was young, I ate, drank and slept sport. If there was a game going, whatever it was, I was in. One weekend, when I was 13, I played soccer for the village U16s against a team from the local pit. As a stodgy and podgy kid, I wasn't the fastest but I had great hands and could catch anything that was thrown at me. It

made sense then that I was the goalie. In the side, apart from the gnarled older kids, the farmers' sons, the policeman's lad, the teacher's two, the boys whose dads worked at the glass works, there was also a young spotty-faced lad called Kevin. There's always a Kevin, isn't there?

Well, Kevin was a left-footed 16-year-old centre forward who only got into the team because his dad was the manager. Kevin was not a good player and words like banjo and cow's arse come to mind. He was not a prolific scorer, more a random misser. He wouldn't head the ball for fear of upsetting his curls and, unless the ball was passed exactly to him, he wouldn't run much either. How we managed to win some games with him up front was a miracle.

Anyway, against this team from the pit we lost 16-1, our goal being a 30-yard scorcher from a blond-haired lad called Max. I thought I played a blinder and made some really good saves. I saved two penalties and I reckon, but for my saves, we would have conceded over forty goals.

But for Kevin we might have scored six or seven. He missed two open goals, three one-on-ones with their keeper and shot wide from inside the six-yard box on numerous occasions. We were hoping that Kevin's dad would substitute him but that had never happened before so it was unlikely that day.

At the end of the match we trudged off to the changing room. Once we were inside we all sighed a bit and began to get changed. There would be other games to fight for. Kevin though sat dejected, his head in his hands, tears in his eyes.

'That was f**king sh*t!' said Kevin, shaking his head.

'At least you know,' said our captain. 'At least you know.'

David Ball (team unknown)

In the early 70s I visited scores of London primary schools in the course of my work – a physical education adviser. While visiting I would often have the pleasure of watching boys playing impromptu football games during lunch and break times.

Typically these games, self-refereed, were played on tarmac pitches whose shape was governed by the walls of the school building, used dropped coats or painted lines on walls for goalposts, had teams of any number from four or fourteen, sported no coloured kit or bibs so teams were distinguishable only by the players themselves and play was conducted through, around and over the non-football playing children.

A lasting memory for me is a school visit when I arrived at lunchtime and a game was in full flow. Limited playground space at this school meant the pitch was very irregular in shape and indeed 'wrapped' itself around the corner of the school building. This point was the halfway line and also the narrowest part of the pitch – about eight metres wide. Neither goalkeeper could see the other!

Imagine my sense of amusement when a hand-ball infringement occurred resulting in a penalty. The penalty taking side yelled to their goalie to leave his goal and come to the halfway line to watch the penalty being taken!

Oh the joys, innocence and pleasures of playground football – the professional game has much to learn.

David Greenwood – Manchester United Fan

I was born in Stretford about a mile from what they now unimaginatively call the West Stand at Old Trafford. So, fate has decreed that I ride the roller coaster that being a supporter of Manchester United means. I was there last week for Porto and decided to buy a lucky bobble hat from the shop before the game. This is now my unlucky bobble hat and has been consigned to the dog walking hat bin. I was lucky enough in my teens to be able to witness some of the great games – Benfica, Real Madrid, George Best's debut and so on. We moved away when I was 14 and it's only in the last few years that I have been able to see some games. It is now a magnificent stadium but I do think the atmosphere can get flat if it's a poor game.

I have a couple of anecdotes of my own from a while back which have always made me smile. The first was told by Tommy Docherty. Around the time that he was managing Manchester United he wanted a partner in attack for Stewart 'Pancho' Pearson. Martin Chivers was a potential target so he phoned Bill Shankley to ask what he thought.

'Oh, he's decievin'.'

'What do you mean, Bill?

'He's much slower than he looks!'

The other happened to me in the early '80s. I was involved with business sponsorship and had arranged for a company based not far from Chesterfield FC to sponsor their opening game of the season. We all had a tour of the ground and a meal in the directors' lounge and were then invited to take our seats. As we were doing so, I was surprised at the quality of the playing surface and said to the sponsor, 'Crikey, the pitch is in good nick.'

A season ticket holder tapped me on the shoulder and said, 'It should be – there's enough shite played on it.'

David Mathias – Cardiff City Fan

Newspaper headlines can often be amusing. One I particularly liked appeared some years ago when a player called Queen, who played for Crystal Palace, produced the headline 'QUEEN IN BRAWL AT PALACE'.

David Mercer – Son of Professional Footballer Joe Mercer

I'm David Mercer, Joe Mercer's son. When Dad went to Sheffield United as a manager they were deep in the relegation zone of the first division. In fact they went down. However, having taken the job on Friday night, he met the players on Saturday before the match and went up to the directors' box to watch them play. At half time they were losing and as he left the box to go to the dressing room he heard one director say to another one, 'Well he's made no bloody difference then.'

David Pattison – Everton Fan

Everton – a true blue through thick and thin since 1963.

At White Hart Lane in the early 60s the mercurial Alan Gilzean graced the Spurs team. It was a wet, muddy, winter's day, never the best conditions for the delicate skills of Gilzean, and he had been having a tough afternoon generally being impeded by large defenders and the awful conditions. Late in the game he tried a trademark flicked near-post header, missed it completely and collapsed in a heap in the six-yard box. In the pouring rain, muddied, soaked and miserable, Gilzean slowly dragged himself off the floor. At which point, a wag in the crowd shouted out, 'Oi, Gilzean, don't get up too fast, you'll get the bends!'

In the New Forest Premier League (in the early 70s – Bournemouth College v. Totton Athletic, if I remember correctly), I was playing in what was turning out to be a fairly over-competitive match when one high tackle too many caused an unseemly melee of angry players to form around the perpetrator. The referee quite rightly pushed his way in to separate the teams and surrounded by a dozen increasingly excitable players attempted to take the tackler's name. At that moment, from the back of the scrum came forth the cry 'Get him!' at which point there was a further surge on top of the referee and all pandemonium broke out. Calm was only eventually restored only when it was explained to the referee that his life was not being threatened but that the tackler's name was in fact 'Geddim'.

David Porter – Hamilton Academicals Fan

The stories emanating from the Accies are legion, and I suspect you may already have heard most of them. Nevertheless, as the saying goes, the old ones are the best. In that vein, I recall the story of the elderly foreign gentleman who used to listen religiously to the Scottish football results, in the middle of the night, on the BBC World Service. According to legend, the deluded man went to his deathbed under the illusion that the name of the team was Hamilton Academicals Nil.

As you'll know, Douglas Park is now long gone, and the site is a Sainsbury's superstore. Anyway, attendances were always sparse, even on (rare) dry, sunny days. It was therefore said that Hamilton was unique among UK senior football grounds as the only place where the names of the crowd were read out to the teams.

David Riley – Barnsley Fan

My anecdote is from my youth in the 50s as a Barnsley supporter and concerns Charlie Williams who was one of the first black football players in England, yet as Yorkshire as they come. Charlie played football for Doncaster Rovers, later became famous as a comedian, then finally ended up working at the Barnsley hospital.

Few people in Barnsley had ever encountered a black person so when Barnsley played Doncaster Rovers at Oakwell and Charlie ran out on to the field he was met with great derision from the home fans. Most of the fans at that time had mining connections and there was great hilarity when the ball went out of play and Charlie went to retrieve it for the throw in. One of the wags shouted to Charlie, 'Ent they gor any baths ut your pits in Donny?' Charlie, with that wonderful smile of his, looked towards the wag and shouted back, 'Aye, but we ent gor any watter.' We, the listening crowd, thought this was hilarious and warmed to Charlie for the rest of the game. It was a wonderful put down and I'm sure the start of Charlie's 'professional' career as a comedian.

If only players of today had the smile and wit to respond in such a way many outbreaks of violence at football matches would be cleverly avoided.

David Sudbury – Arsenal Fan

My story comes from a match played some 20 or so years ago. It was a midweek game at Craven Cottage involving Fulham v Watford in an FA Cup replay. I can't remember much about the game, Fulham lost I seem to recall, but they had at the time a young player by the name of Paul Parker who later went on to greatness with Man. Utd and England. Anyway young Parker was one of the first black lads to make the grade at Fulham and indeed throughout the game as a whole. We were seated in the old Stevenage Road stand and midway through the first (scrappy) half you had one of those brief moments of total silence from the crowd when a lusty voiced fan over to our left roared, 'Come on you whites!' and a fraction of a second later someone with razor sharp wit on the right bellowed, 'And you Parker!' Cue for 8,000 fans to burst out laughing and 22 players and three officials on the pitch completely bemused!

Denis (team unknown)

Jimmie Delaney, of Rangers and Scotland fame, played for Falkirk FC in his twilight years. I was in the crowd one dank and dismal day watching Falkirk Reserves v Hibernian Reserves at Brockville when the Falkirk winger crossed the ball, which was brown, heavy, and wet, to Jimmie who attempted to head it towards goal, but, since Jimmie had little hair left in his advanced years, the ball skidded harmlessly past the post. A wag in the crowd was heard to shout, 'Haw, Jimmie, awa' and chalk yer cue!'

Dennis Costello (team unknown)

I write a magazine for retired PO staff and these are some stories I have collected:

Believe or not, goals can change a game! (Mick Channon)

I'm not going to make it a target but it is something to aim for! (Steve Coppell)

I said to the players 'Just go out and give it 100% – I'm not asking any more than that!' (Carlton Palmer)

We need to go into the next match with all guns blazing – like the Charge of the Light Brigade! (Andy Roxburgh, Scotland Manager)

Winning doesn't matter – as long as you win! (Vinny Jones)

Derek Jenkins – Burnley Fan

I recall a match on Christmas Day 1956 (at a time when footballers played throughout the Festive Season without their agents demanding an extra £20,000 a year deprival money) and Burnley were playing Preston North End – a real local derby – at Turf Moor. The referee was being rather tiresome in the frequent use of his whistle, resulting in trivial interruptions to the flow of the game. This exasperated one of my friends so much that he yelled out 'Hell fire, ref (or something similar), what else did you get for Christmas?' At the moment he spoke, the crowd had suddenly gone quiet and his voice reverberated around the ground. To his astonishment, and indeed embarrassment, a spontaneous round of applause broke out among the spectators.

On Boxing Day, 1960 Burnley, as First Division Champions, entertained Everton at Turf Moor, in front of a gate of 44,232. Everton won 3–1 which was something of a shock. The following day, the return match at Goodison Park was won 3–0 by Burnley, in front of a gate of 74,867. The population of Burnley at that time was approximately 80,000.

Don Riseley – Macclesfield Town Fan

Some 40 years ago when football was played in the old 1-2-3-5 formation with 2 wingers, our left winger was being ignored all through the match and we kept exhorting the players to 'wing it' but to no avail. Then eventually a lovely pass was sent out to the left wing. 'Oh, good!' we all shouted, 'he's wunged it'.

Dougie Andrews – Rangers Fan

I attended a Dunfermline–Partick Thistle match at East End Park last year, the first Premier League game to be played on a synthetic surface. The crowd were on good form and the talk was of a streaker who the previous week had foolishly run on to the park and taken a dive across the pitch. The photo in the match programme certainly showed the burns he had suffered, although what I guess to be the sorest 'bits' were fortunately covered by a police officer's hat! At halftime, I overhead two Dunfermline regulars having a chat. One was confiding in the other that 'there would be no chance of seeing a decent game here until they ripped up the carpet and put all the bumps back'. I wonder what the same two guys were saying a couple of months later when Dunfermline beat Rangers 2–0!

Coming from the West of Scotland, I always find it refreshing to attend matches not involving the Old Firm where supporters are more used to seeing their teams not doing so well and finishing second in the top league would be seen as an achievement rather than an excuse to sack the manager, board and half the team. An example of this attitude and single-mindedness was heard when I was at Ibrox to see Rangers take on Steau Bucharest in a Champions League match. The Rangers line-up at that time included the skilful Brian Laudrup and the portly Paul Gascoine (who to be fair scored a wonder goal, picking up the ball in his own half, before beating about 20 players in Roy of the Rovers style – to cries from the terrace of, 'G'on yersel, Fat Boy!' and then slotting past the goalie). I recall Laudrup being 'eased' off a ball and a fella in front of me taking issue with the Russian referee's failure to award a free kick by shouting, in the thickest Geordie accent I have ever heard (notwithstanding Jimmy Nail), 'For f**k sake, ref, ya dirty fenian b*****d'. Definitely from the school of if your not one of US, you MUST be one of THEM.

I also took in a Dumbarton v East Stirlingshire game

where the most exciting thing was the suit worn by the mascot. I still have no idea what he was supposed to be. The stadium (Strathclyde homes?) is rather picturesquely situated at the foot of the rock and with a lovely view of the river. It is also rather exposed to the elements as one goalkeeper found out to his embarrassment. His first goal kick (drop volley) into the gale force wind resulted in a big bend to the right and the ball disappearing over the wall into the car park. The next attempt went up in the air, spun back over his head and went out for a corner. As he started his third attempt, he paused, thought for a moment, checked and then rolled the ball out to the feet of one of his defenders. I think this action saved the life of a supporter next to me who was blue in the face from shouting advice. The crowd of around 750 certainly enjoyed this and the goalie got the best applause of the afternoon.

Elderly Gent (team unknown)

A few years ago the Muslims of Pakistan issued what is known as a 'Fatwa' against the Indian writer, himself a Muslim, Salman Rushdie. This condemns Rushdie for insulting Allah in his book *Satanic Verses*. He became a hero in literary circles.

At a match in Shrewsbury at that time, the crowd were having a go at a linesman who was Pakistani – until the linesman gave Shrewsbury Town a penalty. Suddenly someone in the crowd started to chant, 'There's only one Salman Rushdie!' and then the whole crowd took it up! From villain to hero!

Fr Joe Breidenback – Coventry City Fan

To set the scene, Coventry City had to win the last game of the season at Tottenham, but they also needed Middlesbrough to lose at Leeds and Sunderland to lose at Wimbledon – a tall order! The following appeared in the local sports paper the following week:

> Coventry City chairman Brian Richardson can realistically claim that divine intervention helped his club stop in the Premiership. Not only had the City chairman gone to church on the morning of the decider at Tottenham – his son was being confirmed – but he had also asked from help from above. He said, 'I had a card from a Catholic priest from Bexhill who is a City fan, wishing us the best of luck. I wrote back to him on the Friday asking if he could have a word with "the ultimate referee" to give us some help. On Monday he wrote back saying, 'Well done and, as requested, one miracle.'

I was that priest. I now work in a parish in Cardiff and all my miracle stock with Coventry seems to have dried up. I have to say though that, contrary to what many of my friends believe, it wasn't me who later sent Gordon Strachan a bottle of holy water to put on the centre circle!

Football Watcher (team unknown)

Lawton remembered asking Theo Kelly, the Everton manager, for a transfer. 'He puts on his glasses and looks at me,' Lawton recalled. 'He says, "You what? You want a transfer? I've been trying to GIVE you away these last four months. You want a transfer? I know where you've come from. There's the door, open it, close it quietly, press the bell, get in the lift, go downstairs, go and do your training. Don't waste my time."'

Fr Peter Sharrocks – Stockport County Fan

One winter's night in the early 90s, a few of us went to the Racecourse, Wrexham, to see Wrexham play Stockport County. We were late getting there and missed the only goal of the match and Stockport won 1–0 but the evening was rewarded when the linesman flagged for offside against a Wrexham player to be greeted with a rich Welsh voice booming across the ground, 'F**k off, linesman – our forwards never interfere with the play!'

Gaz Jones – Everton Fan

As a long suffering Everton fan, I was at least glad when we had Rooney! It reminds me of when we beat Man U in the cup and that evening I went to a club in Manchester where to my surprise someone was wearing an Everton shirt among the 5,000 Mancs – the brave soul! But no trouble occurred though because the club didn't sell alcohol – just goes to show what a menace alcohol can be.

Me and my mates are in our mid 20s and go down to the local pub quite often and one day we asked some of the locals who are in their 30s and 40s if they fancied a match. So we arranged it for an evening in the week. We drove up to the five-a-side pitch and when we looked towards the pitch we saw one of the locals we were playing, a real tough nut, decked out in skateboard pads! We just fell about laughing! He's six foot or so and looks like a German porn star, with skateboard pads (kids', I must add!) on his knees and elbows! Cracked us right up!

George Brown – Rangers Fan

Some years ago I was in the RAF. While serving in Northern Ireland there was not a lot to do off duty. Therefore we played a lot of football. I always fancied myself as a goalkeeper, midfield general or super-striker – unfortunately I was never discovered by a scout. Anyway, one day I was in goal for a game. We must have been behind – with me in goal I do not know how it could have happened. Maybe we were drawing and pushing for the winner – that is more likely. Suddenly the opposition broke away. It was one on one – me against him. As he approached my goal he hit this screamer. It was destined for the bottom left-hand corner. A brilliant dive from me touched it round the corner. I shouted, 'Did you see that fantastic save?' A voice from midfield – one of my own team, would you believe? – replied, 'See it? We will never hear the bloody end of it!' I tried to take a goal kick, but the referee gave a corner. I said, 'You cannot give a corner after a great save like that.' That was over 30 years ago but I still mention it . . . occasionally.

George Ferguson – Celtic Fan

The Liverpool players are at a dinner. Graham Souness's wife says to Bill Shankly, 'I am afraid that one day Graham will come home with a broken leg.' to which Shankly replied, 'You should worry about whose broken leg it is!'

Celtic are getting beat and Jock Stein is conducting a half-time 'chat'. He starts with Ronnie Simpson, the goalkeeper. 'Where wur you when the cross came in? Whit wis au that flappin about fur!' Goalkeeper goes, '****'. Jock then turns to the left back Tommy Gemmill. 'Is that winger your mate? He's crossin' at will.' It is clear he's not happy and working through the team, position by position. Jim Craig, who's on the bench, is watching and thinking, 'Thank God I'm not playing.' Stein finishes the bollocking with the left winger and turns to Craig and says, 'And whit about you?' Craig looks astonished and replies, 'What?' Stein says, 'You must be worst than all of them coz you cannae even get in the team!'

Gordon A E Williams (team unknown)

Liverpool were playing newly-promoted Brighton in a Division Two match at Anfield in September 1958. One of the Brighton players was wearing a pair of very light-coloured boots – unusual for those days. Towards half-time Brighton won a throw-in and the player with the strange boots trotted over to take it. As he neared the touchline, a spectator shouted to him, 'Are those your lucky boots?' At that point Liverpool were winning 5–0!

When Charlie George, the former Arsenal player, first started his career, his hair was long and straight. After he joined Derby County, in the fashion of the day, he had his hair permed – a truly horrible sight. A few years later Derby played Liverpool at Anfield in a League Cup match (October 1977). By then Charlie had reverted to long, straight hair again. The ball went out of play and Charlie came over towards the Paddock to take the throw. As he approached, a bloke behind me shouted, 'Where's your curly hair, Charlie?' The man next to me instantly replied, to much hilarity, 'Around his bollocks!'

Gordon Parker – Crewe Alexandra Fan

Evening match at Halifax. Half-built football ground. Pools of water all over the pitch and water running down the terraces. Teams about to come on to the pitch and the music that starts is from *Hawaii Five-O*! It's a shame the players didn't come out in canoes but it brought a smile to our faces.

Saturday match at Plymouth. Walked into the ground and at that time the away end was a terrace. Due to the fog we could only see the edge of the 18-yard box at our end even if you went to the very front. The match was played and occasionally we would see some players but the only way to follow the game was through the crowd noise. We reached the 90th minute and had not seen the ball for at least 15 minutes as Plymouth were attacking our goal at the other end of the pitch. My friend turns to me and says 'That will be a good point for us.'

No sooner said than a roar comes from the other end of the ground. The whistle went and the Plymouth goalie walked off the pitch – we had lost 1–0 but never saw a thing!

Rochdale has never been a particularly lucky ground for us. You know this when the referee manages to drop his watch in the mud and blows the final whistle nine minutes early. We never did play the missing minutes and we left with nothing yet again.

Darlington away. We had just settled into position and the game was about to start. Darlington kicked-off, ran up the pitch and our goalkeeper ran out of his goal and knocked down the attacking forward. Referee blows. Penalty and the goalie is sent off. Six seconds on the clock. Darlington score from the penalty and we lose 1–0. It's still a record for the quickest sending off!

Chesterfield away. My wife returns from the ladies' advising of a dead rat in residence there. We reckon it had eaten one of the pies!

Gordon Stuart – Rangers Fan

One evening in the pub, some mates and I were discussing who was the best between wee Willie Henderson and wee Jimmy Johnstone. One lad in our company, who knew nothing about football, piped up and asked 'What about wee Al Madrid? Who did he play for?'

Guy Wilson – Arsenal Fan

You may like a little story from a mate of mine from Suffolk – it's best if you can imagine a Suffolk accent. He was telling us about a linesman in a lower division game being reported to the FA for abusing the players. Our mate carried on, 'Wha's 'ee doin' aboozing the players? It's not 'is job to abooze the players – 'a's moy job!'

Harry (team unknown)

WHATEVER YOU SAY, REF!

Back in the fifties one of the best known characters in Scottish football was referee Peter Craigmyle. There were some who reckoned he didn't have an in-depth knowledge of all the rules and regulations, but he did know how to keep control of a game. An example of this was one occasion when he was in charge of a game at Tannadice Park, Dundee. Travelling by train to Dundee, Peter and his two linesmen stopped for their lunch at a hostelry well known for its meat pies before continuing to the ground. During the game, a Dundee United goal was chalked off by the ref. The United team surrounded him pleading with him to consult his linesman.

'OK, lads, I'll see if he agrees with me,' was the response. Peter said a few words to the linesman who nodded his head and gave the thumbs up sign. 'I told you he would agree with me', said Peter when he rejoined the players. 'My decision stands.'

It was some time later that it was discovered that what Peter had said to the linesman was, 'On the way back to the train do you fancy another of those pies that we had at lunchtime?' The linesman agreed.

STOP GREETIN'

Another example of Craigmyle's style of refereeing happened in one game when he was approached by a player incensed at one of his decisions. Peter stood quietly as the player pleaded with him to change his mind. Then he put his hand in his pocket, pulled out a handkerchief and wiped away an imaginary tear from the player's eye.

The laughter of the crowd, and some of his own players, made the player shuffle sheepishly back to his position.

LIKE FATHER, LIKE SON

The legendary Jock Stein also figured in another story that involved referees. This referee was a well-known whistler and was the son of another well-known ref. In one game at Parkhead the referee was having a stinker and to add to the ref's woes he knew that the imposing figure of Big Jock would be waiting for him at the end of the game.

Sure enough, at full-time when the ref went up the tunnel towards the dressing room, the Celtic manager was looming in the corridor. As the ref edged his way past, Jock Stein still looking straight ahead, muttered out of the side of his mouth, 'Your father wasn't much of a ref either.'

Harvey Thomas – Pembroke Fan

As a 14-year-old, some 40 years ago, I went along to watch my town team play in the Pembrokeshire league, against Goodwick which is an area of Fishguard. Pembroke had only six players turn up and the coach tried unsuccessfully to persuade me to play. The match was a predictable slaughter. By half time Pembroke were 18–0 down. The coach had another go at me, expressing his disappointment with me. I relented and went home for my boots. With the referee's and Goodwick's consent I made my debut in senior football. I had donned the team shirt but declined the offer of shorts on the unspoken ground that I did not want the men laughing at my skinny legs. (I had delayed coming out of short trousers until the previous year but would then only wear them again if I had no option).

Pembroke's fortunes in the second half were transformed by my presence as we conceded only 17 goals! The 35–0 defeat was reported in the *Sunday Mirror* and also made the Welsh news on the Monday evening. Surely not since the late great John Charles' first match for Juventus can so much publicity have surrounded a debut, albeit for less glorious reasons.

Sadly although I continued to play much junior football thereafter, I never again played in a senior match. It was thus my first and last such game. My legal studies took over after boyhood, but my love of the game is eternal.

Howard Roberts – Oxford Utd Fan

A few years ago, during the half-time interval of an Oxford United home game, the Club's Community Manager (and former player) Peter Rhoades Brown made a presentation on the pitch at half-time to an old lady who was celebrating her 80th birthday. She still stood on the terraces behind the goal – having declined the offer of a complimentary season ticket in the stand because she said, 'If I sit down I'll never be able to get up again.' Having received her flowers, she addressed the crowd and told them how she had been supporting the club for many, many years. This immediately led to a chant of, 'I'm Oxford 'til I die.'

I was still enjoying that one at the following week's home game, when – again during half-time – a man and his girlfriend were invited on the pitch by Rosie and introduced to the crowd. The couple seemed to be a bit baffled until the guy got down on one knee and proposed marriage to the girl. She said yes and the crowd responded with the time honoured ditty traditionally sung at referees, 'You don't know what you're doing. . . .'

As a postscript to that story, a couple of years later, I saw the couple on Graham Norton's show on Channel 4. The woman told the story of the proposal as her most embarrassing moment. She added to the story by claiming that, as she walked off the pitch, the crowd started singing, 'Does she take it up the arse?'

In the 2002–03 season, York City FC had just been taken over by a new owner in what turned out to be a false dawn. However, the new owner brought lots of enthusiasm and new ideas, including a request to the Football Association for York to play crowd noises over the public address system during home games. This was because York were then averaging around 3,000 fans for home games in the Third Division and it was felt that a bit more noise would encourage York's players.

The FA refused to sanction the request since it was considered to be undesirable. York's next home was against Oxford and the game was pretty dull, with the result that the crowd – particularly the home fans – were very quiet indeed. This was until the Oxford fans started a chant of 'Can you hear the tannoy sing? No-o, no-o. Can you hear the tannoy sing? No-o, no-o. Can you hear the tannoy sing? I can't hear a f***ing thing. No-o, no-.'

Ian Cheeseman – Charlton Athletic Fan

I've been watching Charlton Athletic for nearly 30 years and there have been a few funny moments, like the Hales/Flanagan punch-up against Maidstone and the Kenny Achampong season. But the thing I remember most was at a Wimbledon–Man U game at Plough Lane in the late '80s. Alan Cork, the balding Wimbledon striker, went for a challenge near the Man U goal-line and took up a huge divot. The ball went for a goal kick and Cork picked up the divot to replace it. As he did, a Mancunian in the crowd shouted out, 'Put it on your 'ead!' Cork did and got the biggest cheer of the game. I think it finished 1–1. It was funny at the time, anyway.

Ian Edgar – Liverpool Fan

One of my favourite memories on the Kop at Anfield was an occasion during the '80s. At a Liverpool home match against some unlucky blighters who I can't even remember, a local dog suddenly ran on to the pitch and started to chase the ball. The players tried to continue but the dog was snapping at the ball and at their heels.

The referee decided to temporarily halt the game and get rid of the dog. He blew his whistle, the players stopped, but the dog continued pushing the ball down the pitch towards the goal at the Kop end!

The dog was one of the small terrier breeds and within a few seconds the Kop was at full chant. 'There's only One Jack Russell! One Jack Russell! There's only One Jacky Russell!'

A canine legend.

Ian Parsons – Portsmouth Fan

Reading vs Portsmouth last season. Half time and the announcer asks everyone to look at the scoreboard and up comes a proposal of marriage! At which point the Pompey fans start singing, 'You don't know what you're doing!'

Pompey vs Torquay three or four years ago. A very overweight Neville Southall in goal for Torquay and in a fluorescent orange shirt that is at least a couple of sizes too small, 'Spacehopper on the pitch, there's a spacehopper on the pitch!'

The Chief Exec. of a London club told me this one. He banned a fan from the ground. Some years later the fan gets in touch wanting the ban removed so he can bring his kids and keep the faith. At a meeting with the police and stadium manager, a behaviour contract is drawn up and signed – this guy can only sit in a certain part of the ground, the stewards have been briefed but, yes, he can watch his team. Leaving the meeting with tears in his eye, he thanks the Chief Exec. and, with the police listening, tells him 'If anyone ever gives you any trouble let me know and I'll get their legs broken.'

I could let you know who but then you'd need to clear it with him – mind he tells it better than me.

Ian Scarlett – Kilmarnock Fan

I can offer you a couple of 'quips' that I heard on the terraces of Ibrox when I was a schoolboy in Glasgow in the 1940s. Rangers had a very tricky little outside-left, but he occasionally got himself in a tangle. On one occasion his footwork was so complicated that he fell over and gave the ball away. One disgruntled fan shouted out, 'Look at him – he's so daft he back-heeled the ball to himself and he wasn't there!'

There was also at one time a great lumbering centre forward. After about 20 minutes he still hadn't touched the ball properly. A disgusted fan called out, 'He's so bad his first kick was a header, and he missed it.'

A WASTED DAY

When it was announced early in 1947 that there was going to be a match at Hampden between Great Britain and Europe, I was determined to be there. At the time I attended a school in the middle of Glasgow and I travelled in by train. On the day when the tickets went on sale I decided to pop round to the SFA offices at Carlton Place and pick up a couple before going to school. Some chance! The queue was several miles long and meandered all round the Gorbals. However I joined in and decided to miss school. Eventually after about five o'clock I got my tickets and rushed round to the station for a train home. Unfortunately I caught the train after my father's one, and when I got home I got a real roasting. He guessed where I had been, and he even took the tickets off me and threatened not to let me go to the game. (He eventually relented on this.)

The really annoying bit came on the day of the match. When I arrived at Hampden, there were dozens of policemen all with handfuls of tickets, trying to give them away free! Seems that Europe, just recovering from the war, had more important things to do than travel to Glasgow for a football match.

DUSTY PIES

A couple of years ago when on holiday I went to see Kilmarnock play. My brother-in-law (a Rangers fan) told me not to miss trying a Killie pie. Seems these pies had been voted the best in the Scottish League. Anyhow I duly joined in the queue for the pies, and the man in front of me bought four. These pies were not actually wrapped, they just had a sort of 'collar' round them (in blue and white of course) The man allowed three of his pies to slip out of their collars and onto the floor. He picked them up, dusted them off and put them back in their collars.

When I ate mine it was very nice, but I was glad I was not one of that man's three friends!

NEGATIVE SCORE-LINE?

Where I live the local team is Bristol Rovers, but unfortunately they are not very good. However in the bar at my golf club there is always interest when the football results are shown on Saturday afternoon.

One day there was a shout from the back, 'How did Rovers do?'

The reply was, 'They drew nil–nil.'

Quick as a flash came another shout, 'Not bad – that's more than they usually score!'

HOW TO SWINDLE A FREE PINT OF BEER

In 1946 the first international since the war took place at Hampden, which I attended. There was a full house of 134,000 spectators.

The SFA obtained an aerial photograph of the ground during this game, which they used as the centre spread in the programme for another big game, Great Britain v Europe in 1947 which I also attended (see above).

Here is how the scam works. I show off the programme for the Europe game and I tell people that my photograph is in it and part of the centre spread no less! Of course nobody believes this ridiculous claim. Having obtained a bet of a pint of beer, I open the programme at the aerial photograph and point to a spot on the packed terracing. 'That's me there,' I say.

Sometimes it works, sometimes not, but it gets a laugh either way.

DON'T BELIEVE EVERYTHING YOU READ IN THE PAPERS

The local pub in the village where I live has a regular quiz night. It is quite informal – no entry fee, top prize is a pint of beer and questions are a mixed bag of sport, geography, history, general knowledge – or general ignorance as we like to call it.

One night a sport question was 'List football teams whose names begin and end with the same letter.' One of my teams was Celtic. However the quizmaster wouldn't accept this. 'Their correct name is Glasgow Celtic,' he insisted. An argument ensued. I pointed out that I was brought up in Glasgow and I had been to the ground many times and the name formed part of the iron gates at one of the entrances. He still wouldn't accept this and my team lost a point.

A few months later while we were gathering for another quiz, the same chap came up to me with a cutting from a newspaper and proceeded to wave it under my nose. It was an article from the *Daily Telegraph* sports supplement discussing the possibilities of Glasgow Rangers and Glasgow Celtic taking part in the English Premier League. I tried to suggest that the reporter possibly had got some of the details wrong. 'Well he's a Scot and he's based in Scotland so he should know the details,' was the answer.

Who was this intrepid reporter? None other than Robert Philip!

If you see him, tell him he owes me a pint of beer.

Jim Arbuthnott – St Johnstone Fan

Here are a couple from Muirton Park in the early 60s.

> About a cumbersome winger – The only wey he can get roond the back is up a close.

> And an equally cumbersome centre – I've seen milk turn quicker.

I have been a Saints supporter since the late 40s when my old man used to lift me over the turnstile. I remember Paddy Buckley the wee centre who cam fae Aberdeen FC and I remember seeing Billy Steel when he starred for Dundee.

Jim Dennis – Derby County Fan

I was commanding a small army unit some years ago and we had the temerity to enter the Divisional Football Cup. Our first match was against a much larger unit, commanded by a friend. At half time we were losing 14–0; nonetheless ever anxious to maintain morale, I cheered my blokes loudly and told them they were doing really well. My so called friend then had hysterics – telling me it reminded him of the boxer returning to his corner mid fight only to be told by his manager, 'You had him worried that time – he thought he'd killed you!' Some friend!

Jim McCann – Everton Fan

I've watched Everton since I was a boy of eight. A conversation I had with Billy Cook who we got from Celtic in 1932 was hilarious. Billy was born in Coleraine, Northern Ireland but was brought up in Port Glasgow. He captained Everton and Northern Ireland. He won the FA Cup with Dixie Dean in 1933 and in 1939 Everton won the League Championship. Then the war finished his playing career. He spent the war years in the army and we were good friends until he died aged 84.

Billy coached Peru when they beat Brazil and in his time he coached Sunderland's 'Bank of England' team, Len Shackleton, Trevor Ford, Daniels etc. But one day he told me of the time, while playing in the local derby against Liverpool, he nearly killed his team-mate, the England right-half, Cliff Briton. Billy, a no-nonsense right-back with a terrific shot, hit the ball out of his penalty area but, unfortunately it clobbered Cliff Briton on the back of his head. He was only a few yards away and the power of the heavy wet ball had Briton unconscious for a long count. While the trainer was trying to bring Briton round with smelling-salts and his freezing sponge, Cook bent over the befuddled player saying, 'I'm sorry, Cliff, I was clearing my lines.' The trainer retorted, 'Well right now get out of the way – we're trying to clear his head!'

Joe Asher – Brentford Town Fan

At 86 I am a lifelong sports buff most particularly

football. I have been with my amateur club since I was 16 as player, captain, refounder of it after the war, Secretary, Chairman, President and Honorary Life Vice-President. A feature of the amateur game, not shared by the professional is the last minute cry off. Weird and funny are the excuses given. 'Sorry Joe I have just taken delivery of an elephant at the station and am walking it home.' I suppose Beckham could get one to spice up his estate! Gerry phoned Saturday morning. An energetic little right half, in the manner of Nobbie Stiles, never would he cry off without good reason. Life for him had become good. He had married and was settling in his new house and starting to lay out his first garden. 'Sorry Joe I have to cry off, I was doing some gardening and trod on the head of my rake.' 'Hurt your foot?' 'No but the other end came up and hit me.' 'Oh, so you've got a black eye?' 'No it's a short rake.' 'Much damage?' 'One of them has swollen up to the size of a football.' 'Nasty. What are you doing for it?' 'I'm patting it.' 'Try zambuk – see you next week.'

Joe Kane – Celtic Fan

These stories are about Seville and the UEFA cup final. I was on the LAST bus from Barcelona to Seville that would have got me there in time for the game. Me, my brother and one of my mates had got to Barcelona via Bristol and had to face up to the 14-hour bus journey. We got on the bus and all the seats were occupied by Celtic fans except four – two Spaniards and two Porto fans.

Anyway after a break we all got back on the bus and I was sitting beside an oldish guy called Danny, I think. He was from Paisley, not too far from Thornliebank where I lived. Danny pulled a passport from his pocket and said look at that. When I opened it was a 14-year-old's passport. He hadn't been able to find his so he stole his son's so that he could get to Seville. He was in his late fifties and had got through checks in Glasgow, Amsterdam and Barcelona airports with his 14-year-old son's passport. I don't know if he got home with the same passport – the last time I saw him he was asleep in Barcelona airport.

Another story about someone else on the bus was that they had been driving a minibus from Glasgow to Seville that had broken down in the Pyrenees Mountains. The driver hitch-hiked to Barcelona and left the bus in the mountains.

Also my dad told me of guy he knew who went to Lisbon for the 1967 final and had such a good time that he stayed and never came back to Glasgow except for holidays.

John Ardron (team unknown)

Lowly Workington AFC played the mighty Blackpool from the First Division at home in 1962 under the new Borough Park floodlights. The ground was packed. A friend of mine Alan Johnson was marking the great Stanley Mathews. I had arranged to meet Alan after the match. From the kick-off, the teenage Alan was into every ball before Stanley could get a touch of it. The great Stanley Mathews strolled over to Alan and said a few words to him after which he was roasted by Mathews until the end of the game.

After the match I asked a glum-looking Alan 'What did Mathews say to you?'

'F*** off son it's me they have come to watch – not you!' was the reply.

John Clarke – Fulham Fan

THE SECRET DIARY OF HARRY BREVILLE
(Any similarities to characters either living or dead are purely coincidental)
My name is Harry Breville and I am a Premiership footballer. I play for a team called Moneychester United and I also have the good grace to turn out for my country. Mind you for the thanks I get I sometimes wonder why I bother. The plebs who watch us have no idea of the pressure we're under. Just because we earn more in a week than they do in a year doesn't mean we're out of touch with reality. I bet they have no idea how expensive it is to run five top of the range sports cars and as for the price of a mock Tudor mansion these days . . . This season has been particularly bad for unfair criticism. It all started when we had a little set to with our old pals Farcenal. There was a spat after a missed penalty at the end of the game. You know – the usual handbags stuff. Next thing you know the press are having a field day saying we should be role models. Now to be fair we were innocent bystanders in the incident. To prove the point Farcenal got in worse

trouble with the powers-that-be. As for the role models' stuff that was out of order. Kids need to learn how to stick up for themselves when it kicks off in the playground and on that score we set the perfect example.

The next thing was the 'roasting' allegations. Now as far as I'm concerned the only roasting I'm aware of is when I go round my mum's for Sunday lunch. Mind you I barely get the chance these days as the TV people often make us play on Sundays or even midweek evenings. Now I know a lot of fans moan how difficult it is to get to these games and often have to give up pay or holiday to go. Some sacrifice! It is years since I've watched all the episodes of *Corrie* in the same week. To be fair the missus does tape the omnibus edition for me but it's not the same, is it?

Up next was my mate Urino's missed drugs test which the press blew out of all proportion. What people didn't realise at the time was that it was the last day of the 50% off everything sale at Hardly Micks. Now as we all know Urino is a fashion icon and he was under a lot of pressure to get kitted out before everything went. In the circumstances it was easy to forget he had to give a sample. As soon as we realised Urino had left I volunteered to go in his place. They refused saying I was taking the piss. You can't please some people, can you?

When Urino was banned from the Turnkey match, I felt I had to stand up for what is right and threatened to withdraw my labour. However the gaffer said my playing would have the same effect. I'm still not sure what he meant!

Things quietened down for a while and at Christmas I was lucky enough to get the DVD box set of Rod Van Naughtyboy's and Robert Pirouette's *Swan Lake*. On Valentine's Day we had our neighbours over for a quiet game which proved a perfect opportunity to put into practice what I'd learnt. As soon as I got in their box I tried the 'sack of spuds/toys out the pram' combo. Perhaps I was a trifle over ambitious being as it was my first attempt. Next thing I know some tousle topped Scouser was giving me less than 5.9 in no uncertain terms. Now I'm not one for prolonged conversation so I thought the matter best resolved by something the boss taught me – a kiss commonly used in his city of birth. For reasons best known to himself, the referee took exception and dispatched me for an early bath.

Since then the FA have banned me for four games which has been a blessing in disguise. The average fan has no idea how knackering it is playing football once or sometimes even twice a week. This ban has given me the chance to recharge my batteries and to finish the paperback I got for my birthday. I've only got two more pages to colour in.

During my enforced rest there has been more bad publicity although I can't understand the stick Steen Collywobble got just for taking his dog for a walk. It will make me think twice before I take my poodle 'Becksy' out on the moors.

In the meantime we've signed a new French forward from some tiny club down South. Apparently they didn't want him to leave but the guy spat his dummy out in a way to be proud of. You've got to admire that sort of honesty and integrity. He should fit in here a treat.

John Griffiths – Liverpool Fan

In the early '70s I refereed in a midweek City Police Football League composed of various areas (Divisions) of the city plus the two Training Colleges, CID, and some outlying Districts. It was a wealthy league with many clubs able to rent the grounds of businesses and who invariably had their own Social Club on the ground. I was down to ref. CID v 'D' Division and arrived to find the CID already there, casually kicking a spare ball about whilst waiting for the social club caretaker to return from lunch and open the adjacent dressing rooms. A beer delivery lorry was also in attendance with the driver also waiting for the caretaker so that he could effect his delivery and who idly chatted to the chaps waiting for their opponents and the caretaker. The opponents, 'D' Division, duly arrived but, unlike the CID, were mostly in uniform with perhaps an anorak hastily pulled over before travelling to the ground. When the delivery driver saw the uniforms, he visibly turned ashen. The caretaker then soon turned up and opened the dressing rooms for the clubs and myself to change for the game. Many of the CID lads were chortling and it emerged that the driver, whilst chatting and waiting had also enquired if any of the chaps also played golf. Adding, 'As I have a couple of cases of golf balls on the back (wink-wink) and which I could let anybody interested have at a real cut-down price!' Thereby the ashen appearance as he saw the 11 or so uniformed bobbies appear! I couldn't help laughing myself and the CID captain said, 'Don't some fellas have all the luck! Fancy trying to sell 'knock-off' to some 11 CID bobbies and who he would not recognise as such with their being the CID and consequently not in uniform!' The captain added, 'There again he might be lucky as we only have the minimum number of players.' Also, they were all off-duty, but set against this was their not being able to be seen to ignore a seeming felony. As the teams and myself emerged to start the game, the delivery man and his lorry had vanished! With the bemused caretaker standing there, saying, 'I gather something has happened. I don't know what, but that fella is usually a lazy so-and-so, taking half an hour or more to make the delivery. This time he was finished in 10 minutes!' The opponents soon heard what had occurred and kick-off was delayed whilst some physically held their sides laughing at the whole situation. Thereby incurring a slight delay to the start, as I was also still giggling. As we all were as the game finished. What happened to the delivery man? The CID captain told me afterwards he had radioed in, pointed out their being off-duty, only having the bare number of players and consequently he was leaving the situ to them. Maybe it was the delivery man's 'lucky' day after all! The score? CID won 4–2.

John Haynes – Tranmere Rovers Fan

Over the years the number of humorous comments I have heard on the terraces is legion – regrettably few can be remembered as they tend to be throwaway lines which are humorous at the time but then instantly forgotten, even fewer being suitable for repetition! One example from last Saturday's Tranmere Rovers v Chesterfield match which is no doubt repeated on every ground around the country – in this case it was directed at Danny Harrison – was 'He couldn't score in a brothel on a Saturday night.' I don't know about that but it is a fair reflection of his performance on the pitch this season.

Back in the 1960s, I avidly followed Southport who were in the 4th Division – just. 4–0 down at home against a lively Barrow team, one of our players went down injured. At the time substitutes were only allowed in cases of genuine injury. Such an event occurred and one of the Southport players passionately cried out, 'Sub – ref – sub!' Whereupon someone in the crowd just behind me immediately replied, equally loudly, 'It's not a sub this b***dy lot need – it's a b***dy battleship!' Immediate collapse of ref and Barrow players in fits of laughter. The substitute eventually came on but it didn't make a scrap of difference to the result.

More recent was that infamous FA Cup 4th round tie on 24 January 1998 between Tranmere Rovers and Sunderland which led to a memorable cartoon in the *Daily Telegraph* the following day. It is the final minute of the game. Tranmere are clinging onto a 1–0 lead against our Premiership rivals and passions are running high. Exit central defender Clint Hill – sent off for foul play and Tranmere are suddenly down to 10 men. Thinking quickly, Manager John Aldridge sends on (ex-Hearts player) Steve Frail, apparently as a substitute to defend the resulting free kick awarded by the ref. on the edge of the Tranmere penalty area. However in the confusion the officials don't realise that another Tranmere player has failed to go off. Sunderland Manager Peter Reid and all their fans go bonkers – understandably – while we Tranmere fans watch in amazement. The final whistle goes a few seconds later and all hell breaks loose. Tranmere have made it to the next round. After an enquiry the result is allowed to stand but not before the *Telegraph* cartoonist Matt has depicted Tranmere as playing with a 4–4–4 formation!

John K Grant – Bristol Rovers Fan

In the mid sixties I went to see Rovers play Queens Park Rangers at Loftus Road in front of a crowd of about 13,000.This was before supporters were segregated and home and away fans mingled together peacefully most of the time. I was standing on the terraces about four rows back from the front of the crowd overlooking the touchline. A couple of minutes before kick-off I felt a tap on my shoulder and heard a West London accent saying to everyone in front of him but to nobody in particular, 'Excuse me. Make way for a little one down the front please.' I watched as he pushed his way to the front and then ensured that his son, Tommy, aged about seven years old, who had been trotting along in his wake, had secured an unrestricted view of the pitch.

I got the impression that this was the first occasion Dad had brought Tommy to see a Rangers home game. Dad gave instructions to his boy not to stray from where he was, before making his way to join his mates some 15 rows behind me.

At half-time Dad arrived with a drink and a wad for his lad and checked that he was okay. There was a bit of friendly banter with those in the immediate vicinity and the crowd in that section seemed to warm to father and son.

Just before the start of the second half, Dad was back again. This time, he was giving Tommy instructions concerning the end of the game to avoid confusion and possible separation. We all heard Dad say – 'Leave here five minutes before the end of the game and make your way up to where me and the lads are.' Tommy enquired – 'What time will that be Dad?' Dad appeared to be rattled by the question and shouted back 'Five minutes before the final bloody whistle.' Not unreasonably, Tommy replied, 'How will I know when that is Dad?' Dad's face changed colour in embarrassment and he was momentarily lost for words. Then, quite spontaneously, he clipped Tommy's ear and shouted 'Don't be so bloody cheeky or I won't bring you again!' before retreating to join his mates.

Needless to say, plenty of people gave Tommy the nod when the end of the game was approaching.

John Littleford – Oldham Athletic Fan

Shankly loved to take part in Liverpool's five-a-side games and did so with the same passion with which he approached everything else. International full back Chris Lawlor was a great player and clubman but was also the quietest of men who hardly ever said a word. During one game Shanks claimed a goal which was hotly disputed by Yates and St. John. Did it, or did it not go over the cone?

A furious Shankly claimed a goal. The 'boys' said no!

'I'll tell you what,' said Shankly, 'we all know that Chris is a fair man, we'll ask him.'

After being pressed, reluctantly, Chris said, 'No goal!'

Shankly went ballistic!

'Lawlor,' he screamed, 'you don't say a word for five years, and the first time you do, you tell a bloody lie!'

John Stuart – Celtic/Liverpool Fan

Years ago at Ninian Park, the crowd were giving one of the players some stick, a guy near me turned around and shouted, 'For God's sake, leave him alone – nobody's inflammable!'

One of my father's workmates said to him on a Monday morning, 'I nearly won on the four-aways on the football coupon but the IBERIANS only drew with PATRICK Thistle!'

Jon Muncaster – Manchester United Fan

The scene is Barcelona for the 1999 European Champions' League Final, Man. Utd vs. Bayern Munich. You
know how big the Nou Camp stadium is. The digni-
taries were in the top tier. At 97 minutes Leonaert
Johannesen (UEFA President at the time) shook hands
and commiserated briefly with Martin Edwards
(Chairman of Man. Utd at the time) before catching the
lift down to playing level ready to present the cup to
Bayern. By the time he got to the pitch United had
equalised, so, knowing that meant extra time, he
turned and got the lift to the top again. When he got his
seat he discovered that United had scored the winner
and he had to turn and rush down again. A very
flushed Mr Johannesen presented the cup.

A friend told me of an occasion he was in the crowd
approaching Anfield just before kick-off, passing the
touts asking, 'Any spares, any spares?' There was
bunching and jumping at one point which turned out
to be a tramp lying dead – obvious from his blue
colouring. My friend called the mounted police over
and they managed to clear a path round the body at
which point one of the Scousers going past, bent down
and said, 'Any spares, mate?'

Jonathan Lipscomb – Chelsea Fan

Chelsea v Sunderland some 10 or 15 years ago, and we
were packed in the 'Shed' awaiting kick-off. This was

in the days before shirts carried names (or perhaps it was a cup match) and shirt numbers were generally still in single figures. The problem on this occasion was that two Sunderland players had arrived on the pitch each with a number four on his back. One of them was ordered to change and peeled off his shirt to reveal an undergarment. 'Oi!' shouted the bloke behind me. 'He's got a vest on! You tart!'

There's something to be said for a seat of course, but I sometimes miss the wit and the humour (most of it the gallows variety) of my erstwhile colleagues beneath that old tin roof.

Jonathan Russell – Exeter City Fan

In late January 1967, on the Friday night before an Exeter home game, I noticed the newspaper boards declaring 'International Centre-Forward signs for City'. In the lower reaches of the then Division Four, salvation was at hand. Who could it be? The next day I joined an excited crowd which was double the average home gate. The programme revealed the truth. He was a former Welsh under 23 signed from Hastings United. In the first 10 minutes a long ball was played from the back and our new centre-forward broke free. As the ball dropped over his shoulder it disappeared for several seconds before reappearing in the perfect position for him to whack it high and wide. He had exercised brilliant ball control by catching the ball and momentarily running with it. Initially stunned, the crowd realised it had been conned and erupted into laughter.

At the next home match the crowd was back to its average size and by the end of the season the manager and the 'international centre-forward' were both gone.

I was playing for a touring London club side on a Sunday against our northern rivals Liverpool Ramblers and we had defended resolutely up to halftime. Our stalwart centre-half, a passionate Bolton fan, announced he was leaving the pitch 'to have a crap' (to make use of the toilet facilities). After five minutes the second half re-started without our centre-half and we were soon a goal down. After another five minutes he finally reappeared saying 'Sorry lads, but I found a *Football Pink* in the bog and I had to read the whole report on Bolton's win. Apparently they played very well.' We lost 1–0.

Kerr Andrew – Greenock Morton Fan

At a recent St Mirren v Morton match at Love Street (probably the Renfrewshire cup as we have not been in the same division for years) the guy on the PA system announced that he was about to play a record especially for 'our friends from Greenock'. What he played was Cher singing 'Gypsies Tramps and Thieves' which I thought was quite funny but my view was not shared by the vast majority of Morton supporters who were incensed – sensitive lot us Greenockians.

I also read an article recently about an incident many years ago when Jim Baxter was playing for Raith Rovers. Following some clever play and an exquisite through ball, a guy in the crowd munching his way through a mutton pie took the pie from his mouth and just uttered, 'F****** poetry.' You can't follow that.

Lester Rivett – Sunderland Fan

I remember the time when we were playing Leeds United at the time Bowyer, Woodgate *et al* were on trial for the so called nightclub fracas. The match was evenly balanced and Bowyer was having a storming game. The Leeds fans, eager to get behind their player and show some support, as a jail sentence was looking ever more likely, chanted the customary 'Bowyer for England!' A moment's silence ensued and then the gentle ripple of mirth was heard as the Sunderland wags replied with, 'Bowyer for Durham!'

When Andy Goram confessed to suffering from schizophrenia, the away fans at his next game saluted him with, 'Two Andy Gorams, there's only two Andy Gorams!'

M J Sloan (team unknown)

My mother and I worked at the Midland Hotel, Manchester from 1964–1966 and mother was frequently required to help serve guests at large functions. The function in question was a very grand banquet held to celebrate Manchester United winning the English Football League in 1965. This great affair, for around 1,500 people, had three different bands on a moveable track – all tastes catered for!

One of Matt Busby's personal guests was a Scotsman, resplendent in full Highland regalia, who of course stood out amongst all the dinner-suited guests. Perhaps he had become a trifle bored during the proceedings as he had become rather inebriated and had decided to have a wander about the Banquet Hall. Eventually he was to be found behind the partition which had been erected to screen the serving area from the guests where he tried to engage my mother in conversation as he had overheard her Glasgow accent. This incident incensed the Major-domo who resented the interruption of his proceedings and the ensuing 'to do' resulted in mother getting ready to leave the premises. Somehow, Matt Busby got to hear of the difficulties and intervened on mother's behalf and indeed invited her to join the guests in the Hall. Mother however, politely refused as she felt that would not be fair on her co-workers but agreed to carry on with her job.

Once all the guests had been served and things were in full swing the waiters were informed that a table had been set up on the fringe of the Hall and Matt Busby had instructed that all the waiters were to be seated and be served whatever they wished from the menu – all much to the chagrin of Major-domo.

One of the bands was also allocated the job of entertaining the workers and Matt Busby, wife and guest also took time out to sit with them for several minutes. After the work of clearing up had been completed he had also arranged for them to be transported home bearing as much of the leftovers (wine included) as they wished. His generous hospitality towards these people came out of his own pocket.

This story, I believe, is a wonderful example of the diplomacy and caring of Matt Busby.

Margaret Hopkin – Lincoln City Fan

Roy Chapman (father of Lee – who played for Leeds United) played for Lincoln City from 1957–60 and from 1964–66 in his first spell Lincoln were in Division Two (now Division One) and in the latter Division Four (now Three). On one afternoon, he had the opposing player continually backing into him and he must have been annoyed by this as, towards the end of the game, the Imps had a corner at the Railway end (now the Stacy West) and the opponent again came right in front of him. Roy made no more to do but jumped up on his back and made him give him a piggy-back right across the width of the pitch! The opponent didn't approach him again.

In the season when Lincoln were the first league club to be relegated to the Conference things were going from bad to worse. However I found out how they ensured a gate for their next fixture. Before the game I had to go to the toilet in the main stand at the South Park End. Horrors! I discovered that I was locked in and the bolt wouldn't operate. I started to call out but couldn't be heard – I yelled out of the window that I was in a predicament to two men who thought that it was funny but didn't do anything. After making an inordinate amount of noise, a person did come eventually and more or less had to remove the door.

Mark Guest – Arsenal Fan

My three-year-old son, Hunter, was kicking a football around the living room. The ball hit a glass of Coca-Cola on top of the TV, which then spilled all down the back of the television. 'That's it – no more football in the house,' I said to him sternly and off I went to make a cup of tea in the kitchen. As the kettle was boiling, I could hear a ball being kicked around in the living room only seconds after I had spoken to him. Sure enough, when I went back into the room he was kicking the ball around again. 'I thought I told you not to play football in the house?' I reminded him.

'I'm not,' says he.

'Well, what do you think you are doing with that ball?' I asked.

'Playing rugby.'

Martin Griffiths – Gillingham Fan

One balmy spring evening I headed down to Aldershot by train, for a dire 0–0 draw for the Gills against a team on their way out of the league within months. During a particularly poor period of the second half, the announcer's voice could be heard amidst general apathy emanating from the crowd:

> 'Would the owner of the car with the follow-ing registration parked illegally please remove it immediately. Should you not do

this as a matter of urgency, the army will blow
it up.'

Later, at Northampton's former 'ground' which was a
cowshed by a cricket pitch, at another evening match, I
heard an announcement as follows: 'I don't know how
worried we should be in telling you this, but will the
driver of car registration blah-blah please move it from
in front of the cemetery gates immediately. Apparently
there is someone trying to get out!'

Martin Kilmartin (team unknown)

Some time in the mid-'60s, I was watching Newcastle
at St James' Park. The home side was in trouble, down
on goals and defensive. A plane flew overhead and in
the restless silence I heard an anxious supporter shout
out, 'For f***'s sake, drop us some forwards!' I have forgotten who the opposing side was but not the crack.

Fabien Barthez had an unnerving habit. If the ball
was kicked back to him and there was an opposing forward bearing down on him, he worried us by trying to
dribble the ball away. Of course, he conceded goals.
Eventually, I could stand no more. At one match I
asked who we were playing 'in goal'. 'Barthez,' I was
told. 'Oh, no!' I moaned. 'I cannot stand him any more.'
'What's the problem?' my neighbour asked. 'He has a
death wish,' I replied, 'and I don't want to join him!'

As I explained to my son after City thrashed us 4–1,
'United do not have "defence". We have a "séance".
They all hold hands and we say, "Is anybody there?"'!'

Maurice Purnell – AS Roma Fan

An Irishman, from a little village, came on a visit to England and was taken for the first time in his life to see a football match – rather a rough match with a lot of argy-bargy among the players. At the end he remarked, 'Shure, it would be a grand game if only they had sticks.'

Michael Fenn – Birmingham City Fan

My friend Martin and I are both Birmingham City fans and during the late 1960s and early 1970s we used to watch the Blues both home and away. For the away matches we used to hitch hike a lot and also take sandwiches with us to save money. Before Blues played at Preston, a game we hitch hiked to, we decided to take pork pies to accompany our sandwiches. Well, I remembered mine as I am partial to a good pork pie, but Martin forgot his. When we ate our sandwiches, and in my case a pork pie, I kept joking with Martin about how good my pie was and wasn't it a shame he forgot his. He took it all in good faith and we went into the ground. During those days there was no segregation and I think we, along with a number of Blues fans were in the Preston 'end'. We got a cup of coffee each and made our way towards the front of the stand to await the start of the game. There was a bit of trouble going on at the back of the stand which we did our best to ignore. We were enjoying our drinks when out of the blue an object hit Martin on the back of his head and promptly disintegrated. When we established no real harm was done we both broke down with laughter, the missile was a pie, not pork, but a pie all the same, and I said to Martin, 'At least you got your pie!' We still laugh about it today.

Mick Roberts – Manchester United Fan

A friend of mine lives in Newcastle and he is a season ticket holder at St James' Park. A few years ago he was walking through the Big Market area of the city one weekday afternoon and espied a young fellow proudly striding through the streets wearing his Newcastle jersey. Now, at this time, they had a full back by the name of Warren Barton and this young chap had decided to show his admiration for the player by having his name emblazoned across the back of the shirt. Not all Newcastle fans would claim Mr Barton as their favourite player and this was certainly the case with my friend and he thought it his duty to comment upon what he saw as a great mistake. He was walking behind the lad in question and called out, 'Hey, mate, yer could do better than having that numpty's name on yer shirt, he's shite.' Whereupon Warren Barton turned round to see who the loud-mouth was.

There are brothers playing for Manchester United by the name of Neville – Gary and Phil. Occasionally a song has been heard to reverberate around the ground to the tune of the David Bowie classis Rebel Rebel, it goes like this:

Neville, Neville they play in defence
Neville, Neville, their talent's immense
Neville, Neville, they never play bad
And Neville Neville is the name of their dad.

It's true, you know – that really is the name of their father.

If I couldn't get a ticket or transport to United I would go to Bloomfield Road to watch Blackpool games. One particular occasion they were playing Wimbledon at home in a Fourth Division match and six or seven of us went along. To be honest the game was awful and we passed the time telling jokes and generally acting the goat and annoying the regulars. Into the second half one of the lads noticed that I was staring woefully at the four sides of the ground. 'What's up, Mick?' he asked, to which I replied, 'Haven't you noticed that the ground has a major design flaw?' Everyone started looking at the stands, the terracing, the roofs, trying to see what was so fatally wrong with the construction of the ground. Eventually, after tiring of seeking out faults, I was asked by my cousin what was so effing wrong then. 'They've built the stands facing the pitch,' I answered. It may not sound so brilliant in print but it still gets mentioned in dispatches on our nights out.

Mike Blake – Inverness Caledonian Thistle Fan

When covering a Sunday League cricket match between Middlesex and Sussex, at Richmond, for BBC

London a few seasons ago, there was some confusion among the press corps about team changes and the public address system was not relaying information clearly. As I was not due on air until some time into the match I watched the early overs whilst circulating among the crowd. Sussex claimed a wicket and, in order to be sure I had the right bowler, I spotted what looked like a visiting supporter in a blue and white striped football top (Brighton and Hove Albion soccer and Sussex cricket forming a double passion for many southern sports fans). I asked for confirmation, 'Did James Kirtley take the first wicket?

'Yes,' came the reply, 'and, by the way, this is a Kilmarnock shirt!'

Back in the 1970s when working at Orient FC, we played at Old Trafford in the old Second Division and our Welsh speaking centre-back Tom Walley was travelling on after the game to visit his family in North Wales. Nothing unusual in that but what he took into the visitors' dressing room was . . . a basket of racing pigeons. The birds saw out the match in the dressing room before being released from North Wales to return to London!

N Greatorex (team unknown)

When I first started playing senior football, albeit in minor leagues, I was a naive lad of 15. We had a vociferous manager who used to scream from the touchline, 'Come on my lads – a pound a goal!'

After winning 6–2 and scoring twice, I decided, after the match when I was in the cubicle in the big changing room, to feel inside my socks and shoes to see if any money had been left there. Failing to find any cash, I waited until most of the players had gone home before confronting the manager.

'I scored two goals on my debut today, Mr Cooper, so what about this "pound a goal"?'

Quick as a flash the reply came, 'I'm fining you for playing with your socks down during the second half – a pound a leg!'

Neil Corney – Notts County Fan

This is my favourite memory from the terraces was as a young lad behind the Meadow Lane goal. Remember that this was the era of few seats and rattles and bobble hats abounded. It was when Tony Hateley and Jeff Astle (RIP) were playing in tandem for Notts and scoring goals for fun. Every week this rather elderly and shortish man used to stand in front of the supporters' 'pack' and never spoke to anybody. One match Notts scored and he grabbed hold of his bobble hat and threw it in the air – unfortunately his wig also came off at the same time and flew in the opposite direction into the crowd revealing a pate that Kojak would have been proud of.

Being young, we were rolling with laughter as the poor man was on his hands and knees trying to recover his pride and joy.

Neil Murray – Dundee United Fan

As a kid, I played football for various teams including my Boys' Brigade Company. One day, in a game against particularly fierce local rivals, I had a kick at the opposing centre half and duly got pulled up by the referee who just happened to be my father. 'I'm booking you for violent conduct. Name?' As you can imagine, I looked at him slightly bemused and said, 'But you know my name.' The reply came, 'Name – or I'll book you for dissent as well!' With no alternative, I gave my name, at which point my father replied, 'How do you spell that?'

I guess that at least I learned the power of referees that day!

Niki Hart-Holden – Everton Fan

A number of years ago (probably too many to mention now), my family and I were members of the Everton family club. At the annual family day at the Bellfield training ground, a young player pulled up in the car park. Many of the fans had been swamping the players asking for autographs and photographs but as this young player pulled up the crowd surged forward. This player had recently signed for Everton from Leicester City. There could have many reactions to the number of fans asking for autographs but this player's reaction was humility itself – 'Me? You want my autograph?' This player was a gentleman on and off the pitch and he was missed greatly when we sold him to Tottenham. Of course he was Gary Lineker.

Norman Butler (team unknown)

The speaker at a Football Charity Dinner unfortunately had a slight accident on the way to this event. He slipped on a wet surface, banged his face and broke his top dentures. You can imagine his dilemma when he explained to the chairman that he wouldn't be able to speak without his top teeth. The chairman turned to his companion who miraculously produced from his top pocket a replacement set that fitted perfectly. Later, at the conclusion of his amusing talk, he mentioned his accident and went on to thank the 'dentist' who had saved the day. A voice from the audience piped out, 'He's not a dentist – he's the undertaker!'

Mrs P R Booth (team unknown)

In the late 50s or early 60s my husband and I were waiting to claim our seats to watch a match between Liverpool and Blackburn Rovers. A policeman was riding up and down on a magnificent white horse when a youth called out from the queue, 'Who do you think you are, Roy Rogers?' (THE cowboy of the day!)

The policeman rode up to the youth and, at a signal from his rider, the horse lowered its head under the youth's bottom and promptly tossed him up in the air. The policeman caught the errant youth by the collar and rode off with the lad dangling in mid air. As he passed us we heard the policeman say, 'I'll show you who I am when I get you back to the station!'

There was much laughter, cheers and applause from the crowd!

Paddy Smith – West Ham United Fan

My son who is in a wheelchair is a West Ham fan and the best I can come up with is an example of cockney wit which was doing the rounds when the club was in the throes of rebuilding the stadium. At the time Rio Ferdinand was making his name as a real prospect for the future, to the extent that he was known to the fans as 'Rio Buildastand'! As you probably know it turned out to be only too true in that they now have a really good ground – it's just a pity about the team!

Patricia Marshall – Aberdeen Fan

Aberdeen have always had great goalkeepers – Bobby Clark, Jim Leighton and Theo Snelders, to name but three – and one of the best was undoubtedly the Dane, Peter Kjaer. In an away game against Dundee, Peter was about to take a goal kick when he seemed to become concerned about the state of the ball. He drew the referee's attention to it and looked to be saying that the ball was a bit flat. The ref took the ball, gave it a squeeze, shook his head and handed it back to Peter. Now, Peter's goal kicks were always reliable and he could usually get the ball fairly far up the pitch, often accurately finding a team mate. Not so with this kick-out – the ball never even made it to the halfway line.

It was picked up by a Dundee midfielder. He passed it straight to one of his strikers who blasted it towards goal. Peter made an incredible save but he wasn't going to appeal to the ref again about the ball. Instead of sending the ball straight up the pitch as he would normally do, he punted it to his right, towards the main stand, and right out of the ground.

He may have given away a throw-in to Dundee but he did achieve his aim of getting the partially deflated ball replaced by a proper one!

Paul Baker – Brighton and Hove Albion Fan

My story involves a man who has given his life to soccer. His name is Ted Streeter. He is well into his 60s now but still organises and runs coaching courses for both boys and girls three evenings a week and on Saturday mornings. He can be seen in the local park in Horsham, West Sussex every Saturday, rain or shine, putting out the cones and goals at 07.30 in readiness for the kids' arrival at 09.30.

That is a bit of background but my story dates back to the early 70s when Ted was Player-Manager for Horsham Reserves who played in the Isthmian League, now The Ryman. We were away to Windsor and Eton Reserves in a top of the table clash. I was a young goalkeeper. We were in the dressing room, no warm ups then before 5 to 3, and Ted was handing out the shirts. In our team was an excellent right back or defensive midfielder called Phil Skingsley. Ted handed him the number 11 shirt. 'What's this? I'm not a left winger,' said Phil. Ted replied, 'In modern football numbers mean nothing.' 'OK' said Phil, 'I'll have number 9 then.' Quick as a flash, Ted said, 'You can't I'm wearing that.' The look on his face when he realised what he had said is still with me today!

Later in the same game Gentleman Ted hopelessly mistimed a tackle. The ref awarded a free-kick and shouted out to Ted, 'Watch it, number 9, you were very late there.' 'Sorry, ref', he replied, 'I got there as soon as I could.'

Paul Smith – Aston Villa Fan

A mock memorial card was printed after Villa beat Newcastle United the Cup Final of 1905. It said 'In loving and affectionate remembrance of the undefeated record of Newcastle United – NB. Sorrowing friends are informed that the body will be on view next year.'

After Newcastle got their revenge in the Cup Final of 1924 a similar memorial card for Villa was distributed with the words 'Please do not weep. No onions required.'

A personal memory: I was playing for a London Evening News team against ITN, the TV news organisation, in the Seventies. When I was clattered in a tackle I shouted, 'Heh, bloody watch it! I've just come back after 10 weeks out with an injury.' Quick as a flash the offending player retorted, 'Was it to your mouth?'

Peter Cox – Manchester United Fan

Football and I have never been close. Indeed anything more athletic than snooker has me reaching for the armchair. However, many years ago I was persuaded to make up the numbers for an amateur team that was playing an away game in some local village tournament. I was placed out on the wing, it being thought – quite rightly as it turned out – that the game would be such a total up-and-under, kick-and-chase, Route One sort of affair that I would not be needed to do anything other than chase up and down the line, watching events from afar, and shouting occasionally, 'Man on, Dave!' for no discernible reason.

Then came the moment we won a corner. I was told to take it and to whack the ball straight into the area. Now the one thing I could do with a football – indeed the one thing I thought one should do with a football – was to kick it hard, fast and straight as an arrow. In the day of toe-capped boots, one just simply hit the ball smartly dead centre and away it flew. Fine for field artillery perhaps, but not so often called for in football. This, however, was an occasion when straight striking was in order.

I noticed that their wonky pitch, with all manner of curves, twists and slopes, had been marked out so that from the corner flag I had a clear view of the far side of the goal. It had been set at an angle of some ten degrees from the straight and I reckoned there was a window about a foot wide for a direct shot on goal. With all the forwards baying for the ball – I knew they'd all miss anyway! – I thought what the heck let's try one of my straight specials. I stepped back, advanced, swung leg purely perpendicular to the ground, made contact with the exact middle of the ball. – and next thing I saw the ball fly clean and true into the far top corner of the goal!

Well, I saw it, the goalkeeper saw it, but the referee didn't because he refused to accept that it could have happened. Amateur pitch with no nets of course. A goal kick was awarded and my moment of glory appeared to have passed. Until, that is, some 10 minutes later when we had another corner. This time I insisted that the referee stand where he could see me repeat the feat. My forwards still lacked any faith in me, but the goalie knew what had happened so he was waiting for the straight and deadly strike. Prepared he was, but not capable – the ball duly whistled through his hands into the top far corner as before and I was the hero of the hour.

We never played on that pitch again, the nonogenerian whose place I had briefly taken recovered from his lumbago and I was never again selected for the team. But no matter, I had proved that bending it like Beckham was not the only way to play.

Peter Grierley Jones – Everton Fan

I was at Wembley in the 80s watching a Cup Final of some description. (Unlike the present day we Everton fans were regulars at that stadium in those days!). Sadly, I can't remember our opponents on that day but I vividly remember a comment from an Evertonian sitting behind me. A player, surname Ferguson but Christian name long-since forgotten (clearly not the present Duncan), was having a dreadful game and he got felled by an opponent. As the trainer ran on to administer the magic sponge or whatever, the disillusioned fan behind shouted out: 'Take your spade and bury the sod!'

Scouse humour at its most cutting!

Peter Jones – Manchester United Fan

I was browsing in a sports shop in New Malden (where I live) in the early 70s, when a chap came in and said to the owner behind the counter, 'I want to buy a pair of Glen Miller football boots for my young son.'

The owner was puzzled, and replied 'Glen Miller? We don't have any Glen Miller football boots.'

The man said, 'Yes you do. They are in the window.'

The owner, still with a puzzled frown on his face, said, 'Show me!' and they both trouped outside, whereupon I saw them both pointing into the shop window display, which I couldn't see.

My curiosity was aroused by this odd conversation, and I couldn't wait to hear the outcome. I positioned myself by the door, and as they re-entered, the owner whispered between clenched teeth, and eyes raised heavenwards, 'Glen ****** Miller! He means Gerd ****** Muller!'

Peter Phillips (team unknown)

I was the coach of a team of 13-year-old school-boys. One of my forwards dribbled the ball into the penalty area. A defender came to challenge him. As he drew back his foot to shoot, the forward went down as if he had been shot. Penalty! After the game the forward said to me, 'That wasn't a penalty.' 'What?' I said. 'That was one of the clearest penalties I've ever seen!' 'No!' he said. 'My bootlace was undone and I trod on it!'

Richard Baty – Oldham Athletic Fan

Ian Marshall was centre half/centre forward for Everton, Oldham, Ipswich, Leicester and Bolton. His wife used to cut my mum's hair when I was a kid and these stories are all true.

When offered a sponsored car by a local garage, IM had to decline as despite being seen on a regular occurrence bobbing around town in his Mrs's Fiesta, he had never learned to drive. Reluctantly he did eventually have lessons (bought for him as a b'day present). On the day of his driving test he picked the driving instructor up on the way to the test centre.

An Oldham night club (Henry Afrikars – surprisingly closed down) had a night with a drag queen DJ. The Marshalls used to frequent this place with Dennis Irwin and his Mrs. Neither Dennis nor Ian realised that the DJ was a bloke and used to marvel at 'his' attributes oblivious to the fact that it was a drag queen.

IM pulled a muscle after training whilst in the bookies. Not wanting to draw attention to the fact that he spent most of his afternoons there, he made up some story that he was in Sainsbury's when the injury struck him down. Of course being the player Martin O'Neill described that 'got injured on the physio's couch', this made the headlines and Mrs M had to wonder who he was doing the shopping for.

On gaining promotion to the old first division, OAFC did an open top bus ride through the town culminating in a civic reception and a few words from the town hall balcony by the players to the crowd below. IM obviously did not appreciate that it was 6.30 in the evening and that his audience was made up of families as he yelled down the mike, 'Let's all get pissed tonight!' Stunned silence followed as he sheepishly handed the mic over.

I make no apology for focusing my stories on one man, I will never forget the day my dad (Church organist) helped Sam and Ian Marshall select the music for their wedding. Ian was sat in the corner of our living room attempting to hum some tune he had been forced to sing at primary school and was struggling to remember. There was my hero making a prick of himself in my house.

Ron Garrett – Arthurlie Juniors Fan

Some time ago, Rangers were playing a friendly against Vienna Rapid. It was in the days when goalies were subject to challenges by aggressive forwards – well at least in British football. The German referee, who did not speak English well, had reason to warn the centre forward after one early physical challenge, 'Next time you're off.' Old habits die hard, so when in the second half they both went for a cross ball, the poor Austrian goalie ended up in the back of the net. 'Right you're off,' said the stern little referee pointing to the dressing rooms. The luckless centre forward knew only frustration and anger, 'Away ye go, ya wee eejit – ye must be aff yer heid!' The German ref looked puzzled, 'No use you say sorry – you go OFF!'

Ron Miller – Rangers Fan

Rangers were playing Partick Thistle and it was the first game between them since the move of Arthur Dixon, who had been Rangers' trainer, to Thistle. A Thistle player who had been tormenting Rangers went down injured and Arthur Dixon was called on to the pitch. The player was obviously stunned and needed to be brought round so Arthur produced the smelling salts and waved it under the player's nose. A voice from the crowd was heard above the usual noise, 'Gie him chloroform, Arthur!'

Rangers had been having a particularly poor game

against forgotten opposition. Remember that this was in the days of capital punishment and the nationally known hangman was Albert Pierrepoint whose skill at the job was legendary. Rangers' centre half was coming in for most criticism from the crowd and one individual loudly offered his solution which must have been heard by many of the players. 'They should sign X and drop Y.' A response quickly came from another spectator, 'They should sign Pierrepoint and drop the lot of them'.

Russ Palmer (team unknown)

At the end of each football season I would ask the girls in the school if they would repair any small holes that had appeared in the team strips. At the start of one new season, I gave out the shirts to the boys in the changing room for the first match. There was much struggling, complaining and cursing while I could hardly contain my amusement. The girls, as well as repairing the holes, had lightly sewn together the sleeves and the neck as a joke. I was the only witness but had to relay their struggle to the girls on the following Monday morning.

My team started their match against another school whose teacher was acting as referee. It soon became apparent that, although very willing, he knew little about the laws of Association Football. After a short time, my team scored. He was about to award a goal when a very large defender said that it was offside. He awarded our opponents a free kick. A short time later the same scenario was repeated almost exactly. My team were puzzled but, as I did not allow dissent, nothing was said.

The opposition then scored and, taking a leaf from their book, one of my team members quietly suggested that it was offside. 'No it wasn't!' was the immediate response from the other side. The ref was then puzzled as to what to do so he picked up the ball walked towards the centre circle and, on reaching the halfway mark between the goal and the centre circle, he dropped the ball and play resumed neither team knowing if the goal had been allowed.

My son was about 16 years old when he was training with Millwall FC. During one 5-a-side training session a boy was injured. The coach's reaction to the injury was to tell the lad, 'Millwall supporters expect you to get hurt!'

S C Ruff (team unknown)

Oct 6 1984 at The Abbey Stadium, Cambridge United v Walsall.
Most of the Cambridge side were rather short. Someone said, 'We've got the seven dwarfs. All we need now is Snow White.' 'He's the sub!' someone close by responded. Sure enough, when Cambridge later made a substitution, on came a waif of a lad with long, blond hair.

October 27 1984 at Highfield Road.
My wife and I arrived early and pulled into a car park

near the ground. We had just parked and got out of the car when the attendant came over and said 'You can't park there – we've got 35 coach-loads of Sheffield Wednesday supporters to fit in!'

April 25 1987 at Millmoor, Rotherham v Newport County.
Norman Hunter was manager of Rotherham at the time. When he came out and walked to the dugout someone shouted, 'When are you going to buy some better players?' Hunter smiled, pulled both pockets out of his trousers showing that they were empty and then offered the man his outstretched hands and carried on.

April 10 1990 Bob Lord Trophy semi-final at Loakes Park, Wycombe.
Wycombe Wanderers were playing Yeovil. The referee was an East Asian. One foul-mouthed man kept calling him a 'f****** Pakki' every time he awarded a decision not to the supporters' liking. After a while, someone suggested that he should not call him a 'f****** Pakki' but rather a 'f****** gentleman of ethnic minority'!

Sep 17 1994 in FA Trophy at Milton Road, Cambridge.
At half-time it was Cambridge City 6 Bishop's Stortford 0. Over the PA came a voice – 'If this game is drawn the replay is at Bishop's Stortford next Tuesday!' Final result was 6–1. At the end of the match some Bishop's Stortford supporters started singing, 'We won the second-half, la, la, la!' etc!

Aug 28 1995 1st Isthmiain League, Tring Town at home to Hertford.
Hertford scored first and were outplaying Tring. One Tring official commented to another, 'Of course, our players get confused when there are people behind both goals.'!

April 3 1999 at Holber Street, Barrow v Farnborough in Conference.
I was wearing a Tottenham Hotspur T-shirt and went to buy a programme. The man selling them had a Barrow T-shirt on and he said to me, 'We had a good win at Wembley.' I was confused! He then lifted up his Barrow T-shirt to expose a Tottenham T-shirt. He had been referring to Spurs win against Leicester in League Cup on March 21st! At the same match I spotted another man wearing a Tottenham T-shirt and two sporting Arsenal shirts! Are we all ground-hoppers?

March 31 2001, St Margaretsbury v Royston Town in Spartan Premier.
One of the St Margaretsbury players set about one of the Royston players. The Royston player's parents were watching. The father shouted out, 'If I were you I'd be careful hitting him like that when his mother's here watching.'!

Sarah Burgess – Manchester United Fan

My husband came back from the pub the other night, having heard this from a retired Hibs player, who now lives nearby. Apparently he used to play in defence, and during one game after what he thought was a dodgy ref's decision he berated the ref, 'You are 'aving a ******* nightmare. Whatdoya call that?' or words to that effect. After half-time, things got worse as two, three, four goals went in against Hibs. After the last one the ref, jogging past the player, turned to him and said, 'So who's 'aving a ******* nightmare?'

Simon Warburton – Southampton Fan

A good friend of mine went to a Watford match when he was about ten years old. At one stage to encourage the mighty Watford, he stood up and shouted out in his squeakiest little voice, 'Sting 'em Hornets!' expecting a great roar of approval from the crowd. The utter silence that greeted his exhortation has remained indelibly stamped on his mind to this day and still makes him blush to recall it.

Stephen Thompson – Tottenham Hotspur Fan

When asked if he was confident of retaining his place in the England squad, Liverpool's Steven Gerrard said, 'I don't think any of us can afford to rest on our morals.'

Steve Haslam – Huddersfield Fan

At Huddersfield Town reserve matches between 40 and 50 years ago, a small, dapper man always stood down at the front of the terracing behind the goal which was guarded by the opposing goalkeeper. Two incidents from those less serious days spring to mind.

On one Saturday afternoon, Huddersfield's reserves were playing Preston North End. Whatever Huddersfield had done in training that week or what had gone into their pre-match or half-time cup of tea, I know not but it certainly worked because Huddersfield won 7–0. Every time the ball hit the back of the Preston net, the little man behind the goal offered words of sympathy to their goalkeeper. I recall that the keeper's name was John Barton and, by the end of the match, he and the spectator were firm friends! Furthermore they remained friends for years afterwards. His son was known to me and to my friends and he confirmed that John Barton would provide tickets for him and his dad whenever Preston North End came to play. Full sets of autographs were freely provided and nothing was too much trouble for Barton – all because of a friendship that struck up between a spectator and the opposition's goalkeeper during a match.

On another occasion, Huddersfield's reserves were playing Burnley's second string. This time the visitors were very much in charge and all the play was confined to the opposite end of the pitch. It was the middle of winter, freezing cold and the rain was lashing down. The Burnley goalkeeper was Jim Furnell and the same dapper little spectator, always the goalie's friend, suddenly trotted off to the tea-bar and came back with a mug of steaming tea and a hot pork pie. On arriving back at his place in the terracing behind the goal, he stretched out over the barrier and passed the tea and the pie to the frozen, soaked, but very grateful, goal-keeper! I can still see Jim Furnell now, gaining what little shelter he could from the crossbar, munching his unexpected hot snack whilst all the play went on at the other end of the pitch.

Imagine such an occurrence today – unthinkable, I think!

Terry Field – Coventry City Fan

My dad was a pretty useful player himself, playing for Nuneaton Borough amongst others.

Just after the Second World War, when there were distinct winter and summer seasons and there was a complete break in the summer months, players used to go and talk to the manager about their wages. They would get more in the winter than in the summer. One player was dissatisfied with his lot, so he asked the manager why he was being paid less than one of his team mates. The manager replied, 'Because he is a better player than you.' To which the immediate response was, 'Not in the summer, he ain't!'

Tim Hopkins (team unknown)

Asked to define a utility player, a manager said, 'It means he can play anywhere but preferably not at this club!'

The teleprinter in the Grandstand studio was replaced on screen by Frank Bough who said, 'In a couple of minutes we'll be having a more fulsome reading of the football results.'

Tony Harrowsmith – Leeds United Fan

The first request from Duncan Ferguson when he was committed to Barlinnie prison was, 'Can you get that wall back 10 yards?'

In a match which featured Paul Gascoigne and Paul Ince, Ince suffered a nasty head wound and had to leave the pitch for medical attention. When he returned he was heavily bandaged. Afterwards Gascoigne unsympathetically remarked that Ince had spent the second half charging around looking like a pint of Guinness.

ABOUT THE AUTHOR

Stuart Turnbull is a football fan who enjoys watching many other sports too, but confesses that, first and foremost, he is addicted to Formula 1 motor racing. There are not many rib-tickling moments in F1 (other than Michael Schumacher stalling on the grid if you happen to be a Minardi fan) and so when he decided to compile a sporting book of humorous anecdotes for charity, he chose football.

He lives in Perth, Scotland where the local team is St Johnstone – and if that does not qualify him as having a well-developed sense of humour then what does? When he is not watching sport he spends his spare time on his computer working on graphics for a small band of select clients (mainly his sister).

Nothing remarkable in any of this you might think but Stuart has Duchenne Muscular Dystrophy and needs help with almost every aspect of daily living. MD has deprived him of the use of virtually every muscle in his body and to type even the most concise story for this book required a Herculean effort on his part.